The Dartmoor Quiz Book

...o wrote Dartmoor 365? ...
...join? ...and go two table...
...oor? T... ...does the Lich Wa...
...nlet, near... ...Beatrice Chase live...
...rtmoor's fir... ...here is William C...
For what did... ...rs alighting at Ingr...
...keep a wary ey... ...artmoor's first reser...
did MoorRoaMa... ...he moor? What wer...
of the four stann... ...artmoor? What is '...
What is anoth... ...ard's Cross? Who...
...moor'? ... ...red in a legend ab...
...river is Buckfast A...
...Which convict of D...
...e-Man'? In which...
...you find the Hu...
...stone Commo...
...would yo...
...e 'Sli...
...Whic...
...artr...
...e is...
...d oa...

GW00502104

Chips Barb

...ch chur...
...ecombe, did Be...
...'letterbox'? Wher...
...d railway passengers...
...eye? What was Dartm...
...Man once live on the...
...nnary towns of Dar...
...er name for Siw...
...tor is fe...

OBELISK PUBLICATIONS

Also By The Author

Diary of a Dartmoor Walker / Diary of a Devonshire Walker
The Great Little Dartmoor Book / The Great Little Chagford Book
Dark and Dastardly Dartmoor / Weird and Wonderful Dartmoor
Ten Family Walks on Dartmoor / Six Short Pub Walks on Dartmoor
Beautiful Dartmoor
Cranmere Pool – the First Dartmoor Letterbox
Princetown of Yesteryear, parts I and II
The Teign Valley of Yesteryear, parts I and II
Railways on and around Dartmoor
Widecombe – A Visitor's Guide
Along The Tavy
Around & About Tavistock
Around & About Roborough Down
Around & About Lustleigh

Other Dartmoor Titles

The Great Walks of Dartmoor, *Terry Bound*
The A to Z of Dartmoor Tors, *Terry Bound*
Walks in the Chagford Countryside, *Terry Bound*
The Templer Way, *Derek Beavis*
Walks in the Shadow of Dartmoor, *Denis McCallum*
Walks in Tamar and Tavy Country, *Denis McCallum*
Okehampton Collection, parts I, II and III, *Mike & Hilary Wreford*
Okehampton People, *Mike & Hilary Wreford*
Dartmoor Mountain Bike Guide, *Peter Barnes*
Buckfast and Buckfastleigh, *Bob Mann*
The Pubs and Inns of Ashburton, *Pete Webb*
Circular Walks on Eastern Dartmoor, *Liz Jones*
We have over 160 Devon titles. For a full list please telephone Exeter (01392) 468556 or write to Obelisk Publications, 2 Church Hill, Pinhoe, Exeter, EX4 9ER

Acknowledgements

Thanks to: Jimmy Barber for his intriguing anagrams; Dave Whalley for maps on pages 15, 43, 44, 48, 50; Mrs Cann for picture on page 31; Mavis Piller for page 57 (top) and J. Webb for picture on page 96 (bottom). All other pictures by or belonging to Chips Barber. Maps on pages 80, 82 and 85 all out-of-copyright.

This Book is Dedicated to Jan and Brian

First published in 1999 by
Obelisk Publications, 2 Church Hill, Pinhoe, Exeter, Devon
Designed and typeset by
Sally Barber
Printed in Great Britain by Design and Print (South West) Ltd, South Brent, Devon

© Chips Barber/Obelisk Publications, 1999

Contents

Introduction

There are many people who think they know a lot about Dartmoor, but when the proverbial 'push comes to shove' they are often found wanting, with obvious gaps in their Dartmoor education. Here then is your chance, in the privacy of your own home, to test your own knowledge of the moor, its heritage, history, towns and villages, its writers, folklore and so on.

The very nature of putting together something like this is something of a 'hit and miss' affair because there will be some of you who may find your intelligence insulted by the easier items whilst there are others who will, perhaps, pull their hair out in sheer desperation at what would appear to them to be an irrelevant or obscure detail. We are all different and all know different things about the moor. People refer to me as 'a Dartmoor expert' but nothing could be further from the truth as there is far more that I don't know than I do! However, if you learn as much from attempting these questions as I did scratching my head trying to formulate them then the book will have been a worthwhile project … just don't take it too seriously!

You will probably discover that there is a degree of repetition, so if you work your way through from start to finish then you might 'improve' as you progress. The book covers only the tip of the iceberg in Dartmoor literature and knowledge because it is a place that many have laboured long and hard to study and to try to get to know. Hope this whets your appetite! Good luck with the challenges ahead.

1. Colourful Dartmoor

By inserting colours, complete these Dartmoor place-names:

1 —ingstone Rock
2 —horse Hill
3 —'s House
4 —mead
5 — Lake
6 —stone
7 — Hole Pass
8 —a Ball
9 — Tor
10 — Jug
11 — Combe
12 — Dunghill
13 — Alder Tor
14 — Heath
15 — Dagger Mine
16 — -Pudding Hill
17 —dacleave
18 — Ford
19 — Works
20 — Lane
21 — Wethers
22 — Tor Falls
23 — Goose
24 —tor Bottom
25 — Lady Waterfall

(Above) See Question 11

(Below) See Question 19

2. Unravel the Rocks

All you have to do here is take the jumbled up words which, when unravelled, will be the name of a tor or rockpile. The first twenty are easy (if you know the moor), the second twenty are more challenging!

1 HOT RAY (3, 3)	2 POOR PRINT (6, 3)	3 OYSTER (3, 3)
4 HUG OR ROT (5, 3)	5 HIT TOWER (5, 3)	6 ROOTED (3, 3)
7 NOT WORD (4, 3)	· 8 DROWN IT (4, 3)	9 SIR TOM (3, 3)
10 MR ROAST (4, 3)	11 ERG ROT (3, 3)	12 TELL ROB (4, 3)
13 LORD STEAD (6, 3)	14 LOFT RAT (4, 3)	15 LITTLE WORMS (4, 4, 3)
16 STROKING ALERT (5, 5, 3)	17 RUT FOR (3, 3)	18 DOOR HUNT (5, 3)
19 STOKER (3, 3)	20 POT ROT (3, 3)	

See Question 6

21 HELL ROCKERS HANG (11, 4)	22 THRILLED ON TUB (9, 4)	23 BROTHER MOVE SAC (11, 3)
24 TEEN PROTESTOR (10, 3)	25 CRAB TREMOR (7, 3)	26 THROWS LOTTERY ROWS (13, 4)
27 FAST TRIO TROD (9, 3)	28 NOT WARDROBES (8, 4)	29 TORN DOOR FLAG (9, 3)
30 ECHO RUNG BUGABOO (9, 6)	31 NOOK THEORY (7, 3)	32 MATRON HOWLED (9, 3)
33 CATS MARK NOON (7, 5)	34 OLD DRY FORT (7, 3)	35 LOST ADRIFT TOR (9, 4)
36 NON WISE DOCTOR (6, 4, 3)	37 HIPMAN'S CIPHER (8, 5)	38 OLD COACHMAN BLEW (11, 4)
39 GNASHING INTO HELL (12, 4)	40 EARL BLOCKS COMMAS (11, 5)	

3. Dartmoor's Villages and Towns

All you have to do here is name the VILLAGES or TOWNS where these churches are found – plenty of clues have been given. These, of course, may be extremely helpful later on…

1 Let's start with an easy one! This is the Church of St Pancras, sometimes known as the 'Cathedral of the Moor'. It is in one of Devon's most famous villages. It has a famous fair in September, one attended by 'Uncle Tom Cobley and All'.

2 (Above) This beautiful church of St Mary the Virgin sits in the heart of a pretty moorland village, where there are quaint, picture-postcard, thatched cottages. The village is quiet because it's quite a way, a mile or two, along twisty narrow lanes to the nearest major road. The village, although quite high, is protected from the north-west winds and the worst of the weather by the giant Cosdon Hill.

3 (Centre) The church stands on a hill, the village about a quarter of a mile down below it. Here it is as it appears from the side of Peek Hill. Close to the church is Huckworthy Bridge, a place that inspired Edith Holden whose illustrated diary, some four score years after she wrote it, became a best-selling book and was dramatised for television. The village takes its name from a river that flows hereabouts.

4 (Right) Here we have the church of St Michael in a small place that attracts many shoppers. Its hardware stores, in particular, are excellent, catering for almost every need. Although there were plans to forge a railway route to this place it never materialised. It was one of the earliest places to have street lighting, an oasis of light in a Dartmoor desert.

5   This is a toughie! Even books about Dartmoor's churches have overlooked this sturdy church which stands almost alone, close to one of the most beautiful rivers to flow off southern Dartmoor. For those who know their Dartmoor, the unusual Tristis Rock is not very far away and the diminutive Butter Brook, flowing through the 'cream' of the Dartmoor scenery, drops down into the larger river, flowing in the valley bottom, just a short distance away. The Chudleigh family once were connected with this place.

6   This church has a unique claim – that it has the largest parish in England. (Devon also has the smallest parish, that of Haccombe, near Newton Abbot.) This church was at the end of a funereal route over the moor, called The Lich Way. The village was once a borough but has lost the importance that it once enjoyed. There is a clockmaker's grave in the churchyard with a clever epitaph about time.

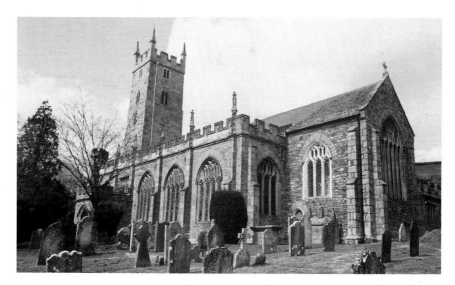

7   This place is just outside the National Park, but only just. From the entrance of Saint Peter
    and St Paul and St Thomas of Canterbury; there are lovely views over Eastern Dartmoor.
    The town is another 'Gateway' to Dartmoor and in recent years there have been new
    roads forged to alleviate the traffic problem in the centre. The railway came through here
    on its way up the valley to Moretonhampstead. Today you can walk north-eastwards
    along the old trackbed for about a mile.

8   There is a lot of 'Small Talk' spoken in this lovely village. Many people come here in
    search of refreshment at either the pub or the tea room. There is an orchard where the May
    Queen is crowned on a special rock capped by a throne-like seat. The church of St John
    the Baptist sits in the centre of the village, one of the most picturesque in Devon.

9   This is a small but pretty village which has its own chunk of Dartmoor named after it in the name of the moor high above. The church of St Mary is on the right and outside is the Church House Inn, one of many in the area to have that name. To the left is a Tea Room, an afternoon oasis for those gasping for a cuppa. Charles Kingsley was born at the Vicarage and there is a window dedicated to him in the church.

10   Some places have names that are a giveaway, this one meaning 'White Church'. The present church is that of St Andrew's which sits comfortably close to the pub. There is a 'Down' a short distance up the lane, which has the same name as the village. A disused railway track runs a few hundred yards down the road. The proximity of a nearby larger town has meant that this once small village has grown apace in recent decades.

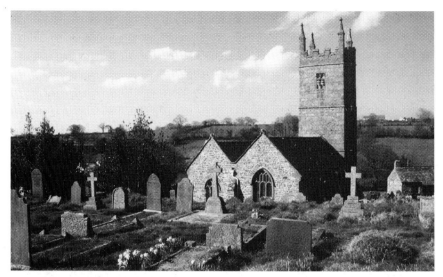

11 The famous Dartmoor writer William Crossing is buried here in the quiet church of St Mary. One of Dartmoor's most beautiful rivers, the Tavy, flows nearby on its way to and beyond Tavistock. The village cross is now encompassed within the churchyard, having stood outside before. The cross didn't move, the churchyard simply expanded.

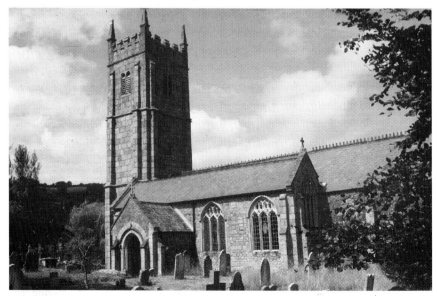

12 St Christina's church sits in one of Devon's most sprawling villages, which is about as unplanned as it could be with a variety of cottages, a pub with an unusual name, and a lively primary school. There are tremendous views over the Teign valley to the Haldon Hills and those with enough energy can walk up steep and narrow lanes to the nearby reservoirs.

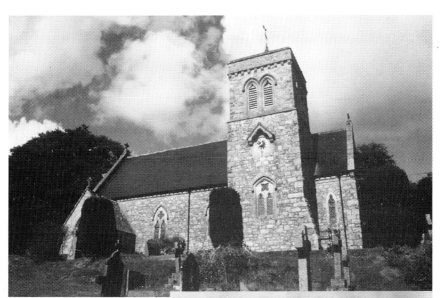

13 (Above) If you stand outside this church of St John the Baptist it is possible, on a clear day, to glimpse the towering pile of Buckland Beacon on the other side of the valley. The church was built in Victorian times and has had one or two famous worshippers from the world of show business. Just a few hundred yards away is the little-visited Blackadon Tor which stands high above the confluence known as Lizwell Meet, a favoured spot of William Crossing.

14 (Right) You couldn't get much closer to the boundary of the Dartmoor National Park than this church! St Mary's stands in an elevated position and dominates the view, when seen from any distance. The village is not far from the River Teign at Steps Bridge and has an excellent community spirit with many villagers getting involved with the annual panto.

15 (Right) If you want to build a church more cheaply than normal you might do it the way this place did and use French or American Prisoners of War. For 6d a day they toiled in decidedly difficult conditions, for this place takes the brunt of the bad weather which is thrown at Dartmoor. The church of St Michael and All Angels has a tall, lean tower which can be seen for miles around but it's not the most obvious landmark, for a nearby mast crowning a hill draws the eye first. In 1996 it was up for sale, the asking price being £40,000.

16 (Above) The clockface on the church of St Peter spells out the message "My Dear Mother". The hamlet possesses a cluster of cottages that have made guest appearances on biscuit tins, boxes of toffees and numerous calendars, so photogenic are they. High on the hill above this place, set on a twisting road beneath tall trees, is a beacon of the same name which has on it two tablets of stone bearing the Ten Commandments.

17 (Right) This hilltop village is not far from the Teign at one of its celebrated beauty spots. The distant tower is that of Holy Trinity church which sits at the end of the Square, just beyond a pub where Aunt Mabel was the publican for a vast number of years. There is a National Trust property not far away, open to the public. The Two Moors Way long distance path passes through here.

18 (Right) The church of St Michael is in a village where if you transposed (swapped) the second and third letters of its name, it might sound like a district in London – but there isn't a rush hour here! There have been various gatehouses here, an earlier version collapsing in 1639. At the time it was being used as the schoolhouse and there were 17 pupils and a teacher who were lucky to escape without serious injury.

19 (Bottom right) There are a number of churches dedicated to Welsh saints and this is one of them, the seventh-century St Winifred. The church sits close to a pretty village green but the pub which was nearby has long since closed. John Galsworthy, who wrote *The Forsyte Saga*, lived here for a number of years and played for the village cricket team. The Kestor Inn, which is nowhere near Kes Tor, is just down the road in a hamlet with a nonalcoholic sounding name.

20 (Bottom left) This is the church of Holy Trinity but sadly it doesn't look quite like this any more because it was the victim of a fire in 1992 that caused immense damage to the fabric of the building. This hilltop church can be reached on foot by one of the longest flights of steps in Devon, and being a hilly county there are

plenty of them! This church stands on top of a hill that is honeycombed by a network of limestone caves and there are good views over the countryside with the A38 not too far away. The name of the town, which it stands above, contains half the letters of the alphabet!

4. Piggy in the Middle

If you are a Dartmoor enthusiast you must have mused over the map of Dartmoor on a number of occasions, perhaps whilst planning or doing a walk, but how much has actually sunk in? The object of this little exercise is to see just how much awareness of 'place' you have. You have to work out the place name that comes between the following pairs from the OS maps of Dartmoor.

If you can do it without looking at a map then you are a true expert! If not, feel free to consult the cartographic oracle!

1. Which cross-bearing tor lies between Doe Tor and Arms Tor?
2. Which river flows between Mary Tavy and Peter Tavy?
3. Which tor is found between Longaford Tor and Lower White Tor?
4. Which four-legged equine hill is found between Quintin's Man and Hangingstone Hill?
5. Which 'fiendish' tor lies between Conies Down Tor and Rough Tor?
6. Which 'coloured' tor, on the side of the steep West Okement valley, is between Shelstone Tor and High Willhays?
7. Which wall runs between Belstone Tor and Higher Tor?
8. Which snake-like stream runs between Green Tor and Great Links Tor?
9. Which river runs between Hartor Tors and Calveslake Tor?
10. Which famous Dartmoor letterbox is found between Green Hill and Great Gnats' Head?
11. Which Dartmoor reservoir is between Bench Tor and Holne Ridge?
12. Which pool lies between Western Beacon and Butterdon Hill?
13. (Below) Which former quarrying hamlet lies between King's Tor and Staple Tors?

14. Which stream, with an extremely short name, starts between Ter and Skir Hill?
15. Which bridge, over the Dart, lies between Ashburton and New Bridge on the road between them?
16. Which 'town' lies between South and North Hessary tors?
17. Which reservoir is the 'Piggy in the Middle' if Kennick and Trenchford are the other two?
18. Which bridge, with a caravan park in the meadows close to it, lies between Fingle Bridge and Steps Bridge?
19. Which common lies on the north side of the River Teign between Fingle Bridge and Castle Drogo? (And they say it never rains!)
20. Which barrow is in the middle of this trio of barrows if Three Barrows and White Barrows are the other two?

5. Dartmoor's High Points

Given below are ten high points on the moor with their height and a small clue. If you haven't got your head in the clouds, like them, you might be able to work them out.

1 621m (2038 ft) Top of the Elevational Pops!
2 619m (2031 ft) Bit behind but affirmatively on the same ridge.
3 604m (1982 ft) One of Dartmoor's longest names, with a flag pole atop it.
4 604m (1982 ft) In the heart of the fen – once notorious for its numbers of letterboxes!
5 586m (1923 ft) Superb tor on north-western shoulder of moor.
6 572m (1877 ft) Regarded as the most remote tor.
7 552m (1811 ft) A nose of land just to the south of the slightly higher Whitehorse Hill, close to Teign Head.
8 550m (1804 ft) Dartmoor hill, with trig point, of immense volume, seen from many miles.
9 546m (1791 ft) A tor just about a kilometre/half mile due north of Crow Tor.
10 515m (1690 ft) Regarded as the highest point on the southern moor.

6. Animal Crackers North

Terry Bound's comprehensive book *The Great Walks of Dartmoor* covers the longer strolls of the moor like the Abbot's Way, the OATS walk, Ten Tors, North/South crossing and so on. But it has one or two innovative walks, including 'Animals Crackers North' and 'Animal Crackers South'. See if you can place these 'animals' in the right place: Fox and Hounds, Doe Tor Brook, Tiger's Marsh, Chat Tor, Hare Tor, Doe Tor, Dunnagoat Tors, Woodcock Hill, Great Links Tor, Rattlebrook Peat Railway, Rattle Brook, Kitty Tor.

You will find 'Animal Crackers South' on page 48.

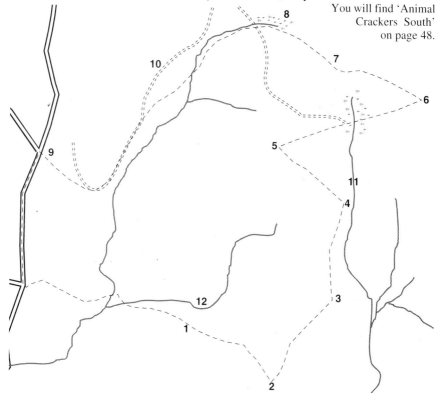

7. Hello Partner!

Below are two columns of things, each of which will have a matching partner in the other list. Match all the pairs by finding the correct partner for each of the following:

#		#	
1	Mary Whiddon	1	Jolly Lane Cot
2	William Crossing *39*	2	King's Oven
3	The Skylark	3	Haytor granite railway
4	The Rock *38*	4	Highest point on Dartmoor
5	Willsworthy *37*	5	Nutcrackers
6	Rattlebrook Head *24*	6	Former engine house
7	Sourton Tors *1*	7	Mast
8	The Gubbins *40*	8	Killed at Chagford
9	Sabine Baring-Gould *23*	9	Ashburton
10	The Hairy Hands *28*	10	Lydford Gorge
11	Swincombe *36*	11	Ice Works
12	Raddick Hill *12*	12	Devonport Leat
13	Edward Atkins Bray	13	Tony Beard
14	Edwin Lutyens *19*	14	Tavistock Inn
15	Manor House Hotel *20*	15	Tavistock Goosie Fair
16	*Furnum Regis* *2*	16	First letterbox
17	Second Wednesday in October *15*	17	Overlooks Chagford
18	"The Widecombe Wag" *13*	18	Engraved stones in Cowsic
19	Lizwell Meet	19	Castle Drogo
20	The Devil	20	Lord Hambledon
21	Tom & Sally Satterly *1*	21	Horndon
22	Napoleonic parole town *9*	22	Foxtor Mires
23	The Pimple *35*	23	Widecombe Fair Folksong
24	Templer *3*	24	Peat works
25	Nature Reserve	25	Hayne Down
26	Lady Sayer *34*	26	A leat
27	Brian Carter	27	Tinners' symbol
28	High Willhays *4*	28	Postbridge to Cherry Brook
29	Logan Stone	29	East & West Webburn
30	Cranmere Pool *36*	30	Kestor Inn
31	North Hessary Tor *7*	31	Eric Hemery
32	Wheal Betsy *6*	32	Yarner Wood
33	Elephant's Nest *19*	33	Terry Bound
34	High Dartmoor	34	Dartmoor Preservation Association
35	The A-Z of Dartmoor Tors	35	Tavistock Golf Course
36	Meldon Hill	36	The Threatened Wilderness
37	Bowerman's Nose	37	A firing range
38	Grimstone & Sortridge *16*	38	Yelverton
39	MCC	39	Ducks' Pool
40	Rabbits *27*	40	Clearbrook

8. Dartmoor Pubs

Try to identify these Dartmoor pubs from the clues, some being easy, others enough to drive someone to drink!

1   This is an easy one with which to start for it has an eternal flame, rabbits above the door and 'Father' salted down in a chest, if the story is to be believed!

2   This pub is another one on a key trans-Dartmoor highway. The Devil is said to have visited it on the same day he sent a thunderbolt crashing down onto Widecombe's church but the money he used to pay for his drink turned into leaves as soon as he left!

3   This pub lies near Dartmoor's most visited tor in a small hamlet in the 'Vale' below. It has a ghost called Belinda, a poor girl who was murdered by the wife of the man with whom she was having an affair. The pub's name is solidly a Dartmoor one.

4   If you want to meet another ghost this is the place to come, for it's reputed that a Royalist officer, Sidney Godolphin, was shot dead in the porch of this Chagford inn and now haunts the place.

5   In most circumstances the pub will usually take its name from the place where it is, a good example being the Walkhampton Inn at Walkhampton, but there are exceptions to the rule. Which large Dartmoor pub takes its name from a tor just a few miles to the WSW of Chagford, but, itself, is not far from Becky Falls, a great many miles away?

6   This is a pub where a contemporary folk group, the Pheasant Pluckers, made a name for themselves playing on Sunday lunch times. The pub is said to be the oldest building in Princetown and its name is appropriate for the town.

7   The pub above is well off the beaten track, in the small hamlet of Wonson. It lies on an ancient cross-county route, known as the Mariners' Way, which enabled sailors to get from the north to the south coast without having to sail around the storm-tossed cliffs of Cornwall. This is a very small pub and it's said to have the ghost of a sailor, whiskers and all, in the style of the original Cap'n Bird's Eye.

8   This pub is just up the steep hill from the 'House Built in a Day' at Hexworthy. It was a favourite venue of Dartmoor expert William Crossing, and its name is appropriate for those who know the status of the higher moors. Dartmoor Letterboxers met here for a number of years at 'the changing of the clocks', to and from BST, before making Princetown the prime choice for their 'equinoxial' gatherings.

9   Above is an hotel at an important meeting place of roads where they converge to cross the West Dart river. When it was built the pub was known as the Saracen's Head but its present name has more to do with its location.

10 This is a tricky one as it's one of two pubs in the Dartmoor National Park not to have been influenced by modern trends in pubs. This pub sits on the outskirts of Dartmoor's most famous village in a quiet lane and its name is derived from a logan stone that is on private property. Eccentric Dartmoor writer Beatrice Chase lived nearby for many years.

9. Unravel these Rivers and Streams

Well, you managed to sort out the various rocks and tors of the moor in an earlier section but now it's down to the streams and rivers of the moor, those things that you often fall in when trying to cross on slippery boulders! As before, the first ten are easy but then they get a little bit more difficult!

1 TRAD	2 NOVA	3 TINGE
4 MEALY	5 MERE	6 DYL
7 WAT	8 LYMP	9 OBEY V
10 NOT MEEK	11 ROBOT TALKER (6, 5)	12 SIC BOWMEN
13 BLAME WEEKLY CONE (11, 4)	14 BURST NEW WEB (4, 7)	15 WOCCIS
16 MR DALE	17 I AM BOMB COOKER (8, 5)	18 OR ROCKY HERB (6, 5)
19 LOOK BRAVER BRICK (10, 5)	20 URBAN HERO	

10. Which Tor?

1   A carpenter, or perhaps a judge, would be happy to sit on this lofty tor on the side of the Dart's gorge!

2   A 1970s rock group are named after this very high tor, and if you look at the sleeve of their best-selling album 'Tormato' you will see a map showing the tor in question, of which the answer should always be in the affirmative. If in doubt ask Rick Wakeman!

3   It's the nearest, in name only, to poor Miss Jay's personal tor.

4   This tor's name was used as a fictional village in the title of a 1931 Agatha Christie novel.

5   In French you might find a pussy here, which could be a talking point, after the long climb up from the Dartmoor Inn at Lydford.

6   Sounds like something out of a horror movie but this tor close to Cullever Steps should hold no fears.

7   The 'regal' rock gazes down on the route of the rambling railroad that climbed to Princetown and is set in the kingdom of derelict granite quarries.

8   This was one of the first tors to have a letterbox, not being as far north as Belstone Tor, in fact some miles south of Fur Tor but still just north of a famous wood of stunted trees.

9   (Above) If you want to see the Ten Commandments carved in tablets of stone, this is the place to go.

10 The Belstone ridge is indeed a rocky one but one of its piles has a distinctly unseasonal sound to it.

And ten more, slightly tougher ones, for the know-it-alls!

11 It's a colour and a drink and according to Terry Bound, in his comprehensive *A-Z of Dartmoor Tors* its "…exact position…is uncertain". Suffice it to say that it's somewhere in the vicinity of Eastern Beacon.

12 Terry Bound says that this tor is situated some 300 yards north of Trowlesworthy Warren House, in the Plym Valley. If we were looking to be cryptic we could say that it would be a good place, at high noon, on a scorching summer's day to help keep one's cool!

13 (Right) This rock is where King Arthur, allegedly, confronted the Devil; it has a ladder to enable those trying to reach its summit to do so more easily, otherwise you need either a rope or extremely long legs!

14 This tor had its own filling station until recent years, a venue used by the American comedian Kelly Monteith to film a comedy sketch. This tor featured in the 1953 version of *The Knights of the Round Table* when carpenters turned the tor into Camelot. The weather was also a bit of a lottery!

15 There are two tors with this name on Dartmoor: one is near Sheepstor and the other is near the River Tavy. Both are a letter short of being an annoying insect, but phonetically you'd never know!

16 Mr Bound tells us that this is a large tor, definitely one for occasional photographers, but even so is not named on the OS map. This is probably because it's so close to Down Tor. Don't shed any crocodile tears if you don't get it!

See Question 13

17 Regarded as an insignificant pile, this tor's name is mirrored in the name of a farm with a notable sheepfold on its slopes. It's not far from Postbridge and a starch factory once existed here.

18 Guess you'd have to be fortunate to get this one. It has also been called Lug Tor and Looka Tor.

19 The name of this tor seems to suggest that it's well sheltered but try asking the many climbers who use it as a nursery slope if this is the case. They say the bridge at the bottom of the hill is ancient even though its name is quite the opposite. The river that flows beneath darts on without caring.

20 This is a tor in name only, and alphabetically comes last. There are the remains of an old tramway with the same name.

11. Water, Water Everywhere...

With Dartmoor's high rainfall figures it's not surprising that it is regarded as the watershed of Devon. Walk any distance on the moors and you will encounter some sort of watercourse. You may be very familiar with some but others might catch you out! Name these reservoirs, ponds, rivers or streams:

1 I am three reservoirs almost joined together as one. The Postman's Path passes me by and I conceal my identity with trees. People love to fish in me and the water is almost 'Christow' clear!

2 The people of Walkhampton live in fear of me for it's said that at Midsummer I call out the name of the next person in that parish who is scheduled to die. I am a deep and dangerous water-filled mine working.

3 Change one letter of the two four letter words that make up my name, and I am edible with chips. Tinners worked near my course and I often hear Avon calling. A 1960s' letterbox was dedicated to me.

4 Tatum O'Neal rode a horse near my mouth and Crossing has a memorial near my Head but both are miles apart. Like the West Dart I have my own stunted wood but mine is more painful!

5 I eventually plunge into the Devil's Cauldron and the NT will charge you to see me here. However, further upstream Nigel Duncan Ratcliffe Hunter has a memorial beside me and, phonetically, I am an important part of many cooking utensils.

6   Where I meet is very important to me, a bit like Berlin used to be in some respects. Do I like 'three in a bed', or perhaps a 'double' or maybe even a bull's eye? My name, they say, means Oak and I am, without doubt, the most important of all the Dartmoor rivers. Queen Victoria reckoned that my southern part looked like the River Rhine.

7   I should be Wet Wet Wet but most of the time I'm Dry Dry Dry. I have my own ghost even though I'm in the heart of the wilderness – that is, apart from the occasional literary Otter.

8   I am a colourful stream and had a railway named after me. Those who do a Dartmoor crossing from south to north will know me by name. At the end of the line I'm a bit of a heap.

9   I am a pool, perhaps even stupid-sounding, with a lisp by name, but a feature found in the Blackaton Brook as it begins to plunge steeply downwards from the open moor near Throwleigh.

10 I am another pool with hardly any water, drought or no drought, and I remain a shrine for those who are devotees of the great William Crossing.

12. Walk This Way!

1   Which Dartmoor walk takes place in May and keeps some 2,400 walkers occupied for the best part of two days?

2   Which 25-mile romp takes place on the first Sunday in October and sees ramblers walk all the way from Buckfast Abbey to Tavistock?

3   Which path, that leads to Lydford, is also known as 'the Way of the Dead'?

4   If you walked in a bee-line from Wallabrook Bridge to Rival Tor, which mire would you cross?

5   Which walk follows the perimeter of the Forest of Dartmoor? It's a route that harks back to about 1240 – that is the year, not the time of day!

6   Which overland route linked the ports of North Devon with those of South Devon and skirted the edge of Dartmoor's highest ground?

7   Which route starts at Ivybridge and finishes at Lynmouth?

8   Which well-defined track rises from the hamlet of Michelcombe and climbs up to Holne Ridge?

9   The OATS Walk was an annual event for several years. For what did the letters stand?

10 What do the letters LDWA stand for in walking terms? As a clue, most of us mere mortals would get extremely tired if we tried to accompany them on their jaunts – but if we did it would no doubt be a great cure for insomnia!

13. Tributaries

Which larger rivers do these streams join?

1	Blackbrook River	11	Becka Brook
2	River Webburn	12	Cowsic River
3	Fish Lake	13	River Meavy
4	O or Wo Brook	14	Steeperton Brook
5	Red Lake	15	Red-a-ven Brook
6	Walkham	16	Moor Brook (near Okehampton Camp)
7	Tavy	17	Baggator Brook
8	Rattle Brook	18	Conies Down Water
9	Holy Brook	19	Western Wella Brook
10	River Bovey	20	Ranny Brook

14. Cranmere Pool Quest
1 Who is attributed with setting up a cairn and depository for calling cards at Cranmere Pool?
2 In which year was this?
3 Which 'monochromatic' hill lies just over half a mile to the south of Cranmere Pool?
4 Who is recorded as having trekked to Cranmere Pool more than 500 times?
5 Who wrote the book *Cranmere Pool–The First Dartmoor Letterbox*?

6 Where are completed visitors' books housed?
7 How high above sea level is Cranmere Pool in feet?
8 Which great literary figure visited the Pool in 1926, the year before his famous tale of riverbank life was published?
9 Which lady Dartmoor writer officially opened a new box at Cranmere Pool on 8 May 1937?
10 Which newspaper sponsored the letterbox at Cranmere for many years?

15. Moorland Miscellany
1 Which Plym Valley letterbox was first established in the late 1950s?
2 Which charity organised its first sponsored walk to Cranmere in 1970?
3 On the flanks of which tor on the eastern moor was there a rifle range for many years?
4 Which famous pair of media stars kissed at Bonehill Rocks whilst making a version of *Jamaica Inn*?
5 Whose Ball was being enjoyed when the Moorlands Hotel, near Haytor, burnt down to the ground?
6 Where did Mr H. P. Hearder, of Plymouth, place a visitors' book in 1905?
7 What number is the Outdoor Leisure Map for Dartmoor?
8 (Below) What is the name of the pub at Clearbrook?

9   What is the significance of the dates December 15th 1927 and June 14th 1928?
10 What annual event is held at South Tawton?
11 Where would you find Annie Pinkham's Men?
12 On which river is Hawns and Dendles?
13 Beside which river is Tristis Rock?
14 Where is the southern starting point for the Two Moors Way?
15 What was the use of Tares and Feathers?
16 What is the Dartmoor equivalent of ignis fatuus or Will-o'-the-wisp?
17 Where was the stannary prison?
18 What was the band of horse thieves called, who lived in caves in Lydford Gorge?
19 Which mire was the inspiration for Conan Doyle's Grimpen Mire?
20 What is the name of the evil water sprite who lives beside the river Ashburn and who ill-treats drunks by throwing them into the river?

See Question 17

16. Rocks of Ages

To most people all of Dartmoor's tors look the same, but each has its own peculiarities and a true Dartmoor expert should be able to recognise this selection. If you struggle on this one then you really should get a copy of Terry Bound's comprehensive guide *The A-Z of Dartmoor Tors*.

1   The tor to identify is the one in the foreground with the great mass of rocks; the River Walkham is flowing in the dip between here and the distant tor. This tor has a pluralised, short form, Antipodean connection and the G & S Leat starts a short way to the north-east. Merrivale Bridge lies to the SSE.

2   (Right) There's not a great deal one can say about this tor, other than it had, in the early 1980s, a substantial metal box to house its letterbox, with its name clearly labelled. Seen from the depths of the West Okement valley, it looks more impressive than it does from the heights of the higher slopes of High Willhays.

3   (Above) This tor, not far from Princetown, has buildings on its top. William Crossing was impressed with the view, on a fine day. It's about the only spot where the white spoil heaps near St Austell **and** the twin towers of the churches of St Marychurch can be seen by simply swivelling around.

4   (Above) One of Dartmoor's famous tors, with the gaps between earning it a geological classification as an 'avenue tor'. It's close to the road, one that has a large car park. At certain times it becomes very busy with the human masses climbing the rock masses. Those with enough energy walk on beyond the tor's summit to reach the medieval village beyond it.

5   (Right) It could be that this is a Yuppie tor in the affirmative. It is a 'super' pile near a memorial to a loved one killed in the First World War. It overlooks the East Dart valley, very close to where it joins the West Dart.

6 (Above) This tor is, as many walkers might agree, 'steeper' than all the rest when approached from some angles. It has the appearance of a small mountain when viewed from the north. It is found on the Okehampton firing range rising high above an underground reservoir.

7 (Right) Not a lot of help in the picture so we had better give you some. This tor, seen from the west, has a triangular appearance. It lies almost north of Shell Top and overlooks the Plym valley. Legis Tor lies to its west and Gutter Tor is to the north west. It's high in the 'pecking order' of my favourite tors.

8 (Above) This is a tougher one. This fine pile of rocks is not as 'grim' as some of its nearby former neighbours. The tor gazes across to Dartmoor's remotest pub, where the home fires keep burning, and in the valley below was once a mine, where the daggers were once really quite valuable, if its name is to be believed.

9   (Above) Isn't it a reflection of the laziness of most folk who visit Dartmoor that most of them seem to have a built-in reluctance to stray less than 100 metres from their vehicle, making the scope of the places they visit a tad limited? This is one of those tors which they patronise, for there is a car park right beside it and terrific views from the top, and the bottom, of this tor overlooking the Dart valley.

10 (Above) This is a hill rather than a tor but still it is strewn with some fine outcrops with numerous clusters, all worth ascending. At the base of this hill is a fine cricket pitch and a delightful Stannary Town. From this vantage point it's possible to see a well-known National Trust property. Years ago there was a golf course around the lower contours of this giant hill. It was the sort of course where you would have been better playing with one leg shorter than the other, at least going in one direction!

11 (Below) An RNIB walk to raise funds. Here it is lunch time high on the roof of Dartmoor and most folk are glad to rest on their laurels before a stroll along the ridge to an even slightly higher point.

12 (Right) This tor has a colour in its name, has a wood of stunted oaks named after it, is near a reservoir which supplies North Devon, and is on a firing range.

13 (Above) Who needs any clues to this one? For many visitors it is the only tor on the moor that they ever climb!

14 Here is Dartmoor's oldest reservoir looking from a point near a former railway line. The tor that has to be identified is one beyond (if you'll excuse the language) the dam wall!

This extremely rock-capped hill possesses a 'cave' on its side where a character called Elford avoided capture when being pursued during the English Civil War.

15 (Right) If you stand on Sheepstor, a fine rockpile and a favourite haunt of the pixies, you look across the top of Burrator Reservoir to a hill capped with more tors. The one we want you to identify is the triangular mass on the right side of the picture. And if you are having problems with this one, don't get 'real het' up about it!

16 At the conglomeration of buildings in the snowy picture above there once lived a community of workers involved in the manufacture of gunpowder from 1844 to 1872. The picture is taken from the B3212 so all you have to do is to identify the outcrop on the hillside beyond the buildings.

17 (Right) This Plym valley tor has been quarried for its pinky-red granites. Indeed there is a cylinder-shaped rock there from long ago which was hewn and shaped to be the base for a flagpole at Devonport Docks but was never hauled away. Perhaps the most trivial fact gleaned from Terry Bound's *A-Z of Dartmoor Tors* is that the line of longitude four degrees west passes through the tor!

18 (Above) If you have ever walked to this tor you will appreciate why those who know the moor regard this as the most remote rockpile of them all. To the south is a great peat fen, almost featureless and quite flat, for Dartmoor. To the west one of Dartmoor's most spectacular rivers wends its way off the moor through a steep-sided valley. To the north there is more peat and a plateau on which many of Dartmoor's rivers rise, some flowing southwards, others heading for the celtic kingdoms to the north.

19 (Right) We all have a cross to bear, as does this tor, this one commemorating the Golden Jubilee of good Queen Victoria. The tor has changed its name bit by bit. When it was without the final 't', climbing it was an uplifting experience but now it's just a spoilt child. Say no more!

20 (Below) The pile of rocks to be named is the one on the left. These outcrops overlook Widecombe and this location has been used for numerous films. The nearest tor sounds strangely familiar and its name rings true, hopefully.

17. Past Industries – Gone but Not Forgotten?

1 What was an alternative name for the small copper mine, Walkhampton Consols?
2 What was manufactured, in trenches, on the north side of Sourton Tors, for a few years in the second half of the nineteenth century?
3 Which substance, derived from iron ore and used mainly in paint manufacture, was produced at Ashburton from the 1870s to just after the turn of the century? It also occurred in the hills and cliffs near Brixham.
4 Which valuable substance occurs at Hemerdon, near Plympton? It has various uses including the toughening of steel.
5 Which canal did John Taylor engineer to convey minerals, originated from the Mary Tavy area, down to the navigable Tamar?
6 Which important copper mine, near Mary Tavy, covered some 30 acres and went to a depth of more than 1300 feet beneath the surface? It also went under parts of the main Okehampton–Tavistock road and there are extensive surface remains of this disused mine still visible.
7 Near the head of which brook were the Henroost and Hooten Wheels mines?
8 What type of gas was manufactured using peat?
9 What industry was established near Cherry Brook, by Mr Frean, in 1844?
10 What is the name of the trough that carries water to the top of a waterwheel?

18. Who Am I?

1 I am a farmer who farms near Widecombe. Over the years people have come to know my distinctive Devonshire accent as I have built a career out of entertaining people. I have a request show on local radio and have made many television appearances. Telling amusing and humorous dialect stories is another thing that I enjoy doing.

2 I lie at rest in the graveyard at Chagford church. I was a noted guide and fisherman in the days of Queen Victoria and I set up a cairn at Cranmere Pool.

3 I have written several best-selling novels, the first not until I was more than 70 years old. Several of them have been dramatised for television. I used to live on Dartmoor, near Chagford, but moved to Totnes. My surname is the same as a former hymn writer and preacher.

4 People prefer to label me 'notorious' rather than famous for my criminal activities with an axe. I escaped from Dartmoor Prison and although my clothes were found at Crockernwell, on the Exeter to Okehampton road, I was never seen again!

5 (Right) I was inspired to write works of fiction, particularly after staying at the Duchy Hotel in Princetown. For a while I was a doctor in Plymouth but although I was not 'hounded' out of town I left the area. Here is a picture of me.

See Question 5

6 I am the grandfather of Lady Sylvia Sayer and shared with her the most profound love and respect for the beauties of Dartmoor. Although I lived, and died, a great many years ago people will probably have seen some of the books I wrote and photographs that I took.

7 Among my triumphs was the courting of a Chagford girl whose parents owned a hotel in the town. At times when accommodation was limited I occasionally pitched a tent on the lawn. However this was half a world away from my roots – there are no kangaroos in Chagford, sport! I have been back to Devon many times, starring in pantomimes and for family visits.

8 I walked on Dartmoor in the mid 1920s visiting some of the loneliest, most inaccessible spots, places like Cranmere Pool. This was a place that I mentioned in one of my most famous works of fiction, one which has also given its name to a long distance walk that meanders across that great rolling landscape between Dartmoor and the North Devon Coast. That story was also made into a film.

9 I visited Devon many times, staying with friends at Haldon House and also at Chagford. I had intended doing some experiments from Meldon Hill, above this ancient stannary town, but some of my greatest efforts were reserved for the cliffs above Poldhu in Cornwall, better placed to 'bridge' the Atlantic.

10 I shared a love scene with the lovely Jane Seymour at Bonehill Rocks, high above Widecombe. We all knew that *Jamaica Inn* should have been filmed in Cornwall but Dartmoor was more suitable for our visual needs. The decision had nothing to do with making the film on a 'Shoestring'.

11 Fishing the Dartmoor rivers was always a passion for me and many years of my life were spent in Devon, as I grew up at Jordan, near Widecombe. When Harry Secombe made a *Highway* programme about Dartmoor we filmed me fishing in the East Dart near Bellever and talked about my long career as a stage, television and film actor. I enjoyed a long life, having been born in 1911, and was honoured with a knighthood. You may have seen me in many things, *El Cid, Genghis Khan, Khartoum, Where Eagles Dare* and even *Up Pompeii* with Frankie Howerd.

12   You have been to Princetown? Lovely, isn't it? Well you can really thank me because I was the man with the late eighteenth century vision to try to develop Dartmoor as an agricultural area and this was my 'patch', so to speak. True, it wasn't a great success, but when French POWs needed to be accommodated I was there backing Princetown all the way. I was a personal friend of the Prince of Wales and in a distinguished career held many posts, just one of them being Lord Warden of the Stannaries.

13   Have you been to see my granite tramway that skirts Haytor Down? People always remember my contribution to industry but they forget that I was the Master of the South Devon foxhounds, a poet and a man of great learning even though I was no 'saint'.

14   When I was alive I was proud to have entertained so many good 'folk'. My Pixie Band played all over the county and local folk music was a real passion for me. I lived at South Tawton and I initiated the annual Dartmoor Pixie Folk festival.

See Question 14

15   I made a series of documentaries for Westward Television many years ago when I lived in the Tavistock area. Devon is a place I know well, having walked much of the coast-line, worked as a carpenter at a holiday camp in Brixham, and also as a steward on the passenger ferry from Torquay to Brixham. Since leaving the county I have made many more documentaries for HTV.

16   Most people would imagine that I may have been a bit a saddle sore for over a period of fifty years, in the eighteenth century, I travelled the length and breadth of the country on horseback preaching 40,000 sermons to people. I was well received at Sticklepath on the edge of the moor but also faced less friendly souls at Tiverton and Plymouth from time to time.

17   For a while I lived in Torquay and enjoyed the delights of Devon. Friends of mine kept a hotel in Moretonhampstead and so I often visited them there. People will remember some of my catch phrases and despite what they say, I was never obsessed by wanting doors shut!

18   I played cricket for the MCC, which sounds rather grand but I should explain that this is Manaton Cricket Club! I was never a successful batsman but loved the game nevertheless. Whilst I was here I wrote short stories and plays and loved riding the moors on horseback. I would pass Jay's Grave and this inspired me to write a short story called 'The Apple Tree'. Many years after my death, in 1933, this was made into a fine film called *A Summer Story*.

19   I was a detective with Scotland Yard but on retirement sought the quieter pastures of living on Dartmoor. I moved to Haytor Vale, continued my Dartmoor education, taught classes about the moor and its history. I also wrote a number of Dartmoor books, mostly in the 1980s. After my death those who knew me recognised my contribution to the cause and very kindly placed an appropriate memorial to me on the moor in the shape of a restored clapper bridge on the North Teign river.

20   The cross I erected bears my name. My son Frederic J. had his initials adopted for cars registered at Exeter, and both of us were keen landscape artists. The Lydford House Hotel is, I believe, a nice place for some light refreshments ... but I would say that as it used to be my home!

19. Dartmoor Definitions

Below are given a number of definitions of words and terms associated with Dartmoor. Working the other way round, come up with the right words. As usual, some are obscure, others even more so! To help out, the number of letters in the answer is in brackets.

1 Normally a body of static water but on Dartmoor invariably moving as in various examples like RED, FISH, and DARK. (4)
2 A steep-sided valley like those found at Lustleigh, Belstone and at places along the Tavy. (6)
3 The Celtic translation of the two syllables of this word are table and stone. Spinsters Rock is a good example. (6)
4 Larger than a gulley, but starting with the same initial letter. A deep open mine working. (4)
5 Probably the most obscure word here, this one also applies to a steep gulley. Water was often carried away through them from mine workings. According to William Crossing there was a good example on the slope of Gibbet Hill leading down to the Cholwell Brook. (6)
6 A quantity of peat, as much as could be cut from a length of some forty yards and twice the width of the turving iron. Two of these made for a good day's work and an even better night's sleep! (7)
7 The representatives at the Tinners' Parliament. (6)
8 A large stone that is or was so delicately balanced that weight applied to certain points could cause a rock of many tons to rock to and fro on its pivot. The Nutcrackers in Lustleigh Cleave and the Rugglestone near Widecombe were good examples. (5,6)
9 The term applied to the earliest tinners on Dartmoor. (3,3,3)
10 Areas of land, usually about eight acres, enclosing bits of moorland for farming purposes, many being created in the late eighteenth/early nineteenth centuries. (8)
11 A circumnavigation of the bounds of the Forest of Dartmoor made by order of Henry III. (13)
12 A man elected at the Duchy Court to perform duties associated with commoners' rights, and cattle drifts. (5)
13 The practice, often misused these days, of being able to build a house in a day, twixt sunrise and sunset, and the property and lands enclosed could be claimed by the builder, as happened at Jolly Lane Cot in the 1830s when Tom and Sally Satterly took advantage of this custom. (9,6)
14 This is a quaint term and almost cryptic in a way. It is a term for Dartmoor mires probably so named because of the numbers of four-legged friends to become stuck in them! (8,7)
15 The burning of furze and heather to enable new grass to sprout so that cattle may have good grazing. (7)
16 A stone with a hole in it, the two components of the answer meaning 'holed' and 'stone', there being a fine one beside the North Teign river near Scorhill. (6)
17 The right of commoners and forest tenants to cut peat. (7)
18 The name often given to commons or small downs on the southern Dartmoor. Dendles and Yadsworthy are examples. (5)
19 A berry that grows in great abundance on Dartmoor, in July and August. Its Latin name is *Vaccinium myrtillus*. (12)
20 Land set apart for the preservation of game. In particular the breeding of rabbits has been their main use in many parts of the moor. (6)

20. Another Moorland Miscellany

1 Which bridge is crossed when driving between the Warren House Inn and Merripit Hill?
2 At which former railway station was Jumbo, the station cat, supposedly buried?
3 Where would you find the words '*Parcere Subjectis*'?
4 What, so it's said, never goes out at the Warren House Inn?
5 Which river passes under Postbridge's clapper bridge?
6 What was once the Dartmoor home of Lord Hambledon?
7 Which 'station' carried a warning for people to beware of snakes?
8 Apart from Kitty Jay, which other suicide victim is buried at a lonely crossroads on the moor?
9 What is the highest point on Southern Dartmoor?
10 Where would you find a White Rajah of Sarawak buried?
11 Near which moorland village was Great Week Mine?
12 What was the name of the mill owned by William Crossing's family at South Brent?
13 If Wistman's Wood and Black Tor Copse are two out of a trio what is the third?
14 Which warren extended from the boundary of Legis Tor Warren to Combshead,
. Eylesbarrow and Evil Combe in the Plym valley?
15 Which television comedy actor has played cricket for Chagford?
16 Where was Stowford Mill?
17 Which rock group of the seventies made an album called 'Tormato' with a map of the Yes Tor area on the sleeve?
18 On the side of which valley is Hen Tor?
19 Where were 'the Nutcrackers'?
20 In which village is the pub called 'The White Thorn'?

21. Dartmoor Name Game

Complete these Dartmoor place names – the number of letters required is shown in brackets:

1 Buckland (6)	2 Staldon (6)
3 Cold East (5)	4 Hangershell (4)
5 Swelltor (8)	6 Tiger's (5)
7 Browne's (5)	8 Seven Lords' (5)
9 (5) Trowlesworthy (3)	10 Cadover (6)
11 Fish (4)	12 Cranmere (4)
13 Ringmoor (6)	14 Hawns and (7)
15 Widgery (5)	16 Great Links (3)
17 Bleak (5)	18 Roborough (4)
19 Huckworthy (6)	20 Cut Combe (5)
21 Shilley (4)	22 The Nine (7)
23 Becky (5)	24 Bowerman's (4)
25 Jay's (5)	26 Hameldown (6)
27 Meldon (9)	28 Cripdon (4)
29 Lustleigh (6)	30 Tristis (4)
31 Gibbet (4)	32 Fernworthy (9)
33 Wind (3)	34 Bonehill (5)
35 Becka (5)	36 Burrator (9)
37 Shell (3)	38 Hanger (4)
39 Cullever (5)	40 Stephens' (5)

22. Dartmoor's Past Industries

What was produced/extracted/processed or manufactured at the following places?

1 In the vicinity of Bleak House
2 Red Lake
3 Shipley Bridge
4 Meldon
5 Lee Moor
6 Merrivale
7 Sourton
8 Golden Dagger
9 Yarner
10 Powder Mills

23. Nineteenth Century Dartmoor

1 In which valley was Knock Mine?
2 Which vicar inscribed stones in and around the Cowsic River near Two Bridges?
3 Where did the Duke brothers own a quarry?
4 Which farm near Postbridge, destroyed by fire on 3 January 1907, was the home of the Cleave family?
5 How is the Dartmoor Depot, established in 1808, better known today?
6 When Prince Albert visited Brimpts, near Dartmeet, in 1846 he heard a distant gunfire salute as Queen Victoria arrived at another place in Devon. Where?
7 Who was the famous vicar of Lewtrenchard who collected folksongs and ballads?
8 What happened to three soldiers of the 7th Royal Fusiliers in 1853 whilst on their way from Dousland to Princetown?
9 What paralysed life on the moor after 8 March 1891?
10 Which Dartmoor reservoir was completed in September 1898?
11 In which year was the Dartmoor Preservation Association formed?
12 Which inn, usually associated with the tin mining industry, was built in 1845 to replace one which stood opposite and was known as Newhouse?
13 Which mine, that finally closed in the 1870s, was sited close to the confluence of the rivers Walkham and Tavy and named after the spinster Queen Elizabeth I?
14 Which mine, now remembered in its engine house, reopened in 1806 to produce lead and copper and also arsenic and silver?
15 What did Mr Lamb keep on the moor?
16 Which city, in the 1890s, paved its streets and kerbs with vast amounts of granite from Yeo near Chagford?
17 Which settlement developed following the excavation of china clay from a number of pits between Cadover Bridge and Crownhill Down?
18 At the head of which brook, a tributary of the Avon, would you have found two clay workings known as Hall's Pit and Hill's Pit, after the men who started them?
19 What industrial enterprise, involving peat, did Jacob Hall Drew and Peter Adams start at Bachelor's Hall, near Princetown, in 1844?
20 At the head of which stream did the West of England Compressed Peat Company Ltd carry out their operations?

24. 'Moor' Dartmoor Names

Fifty names that need to be completed – you have probably seen most of them on the map at some time but did they register?

1 Corringdon (4)	2 Buckland (6)
3 Left (4)	4 Leedon (4)
5 Leeper (5)	6 Annie (8, 3)
7 Badger's (4)	8 Belford (4)
9 Yellowmead (4)	10 Zeal (3, 7)
11 Yadsworthy (5)	12 Wooston (6)
13 Willingstone (4)	14 Headland (6)
15 (5) Dunghill	16 Bloody (4)
17 Bradmere or Bradford (4)	18 (8) Gulf
19 Canna (4)	20 Cave- (6) Memorial
21 (5, 2) Gold	22 Smallbrook (6)
23 Seven (5, 5)	24 Hoo (5)
25 Hortonsford (6)	26 Horsham (5)
27 Yennadon (5)	28 (4) Wethers
29 Glassy (5)	30 Sandy (4, 4)
31 Grant's (3)	32 Grim's (5)
33 Gobbet (4)	34 Gibby (4)
35 Cater's (4)	36 Gallant (2, 5)
37 Sampford (6)	38 Herring's (5)
39 Fitz's (4)	40 Estrayer (4)
41 Goldsmith's (5)	42 Chinkwell (3)
43 Devonport (4)	44 Delamore (5)
45 Fatherford (7)	46 Elephant's (4)
47 Foale's (8)	48 Lydia (6)
49 Nun's (5, 4)	50 Powder (5)

25. What's in a Picture?

This section is one of 16 pictures with 6 questions about each one and those of you who are good at maths will know that this yields 96 answers. To make it up to a round hundred four additional questions are added, based on your observations of all the pictures. Don't worry, it will all be as clear as the ooze in a Dartmoor mire ...

1　What's the name of this inscribed stone?
2　Beside which river does it stand?
3　Into which bay does this river flow?
4　What is the river's alternative name?
5　What is the name of the nearby bridge?
6　Which former house stood just up the road from here?

7　Which Dartmoor bridge is this?
8　Which river does it span?
9　Which Dartmoor attraction lies a short distance down-stream?
10　What is the nearest 'tin town' to this bridge?
11　Which immense wood covers a vast acreage in this river valley?
12　What is the next bridge upstream?

(Right)
13 What is the name of this famous beauty spot?
14 Which river does the bridge span?
15 Which 'stannary' town lies a few miles upstream?
16 What is the name of the pub beside the bridge on the
    north bank of the river?
17 What is the name of the next road bridge downstream?
18 What's the name of the next road bridge upstream?

(Below)
19 Which 'skeletal rocks' are shown here?
20 What are the two closest tors to this pile?

21 Which village lies in the valley below this outcrop?
22 Which river runs through this 'broad valley'?
23 Which two stars had a romantic embrace at these rocks when making a film version of
    Jamaica Inn?
24 Which *Pride and Prejudice* 'heart-throb' filmed several shots here for a Ruth Rendell
    Mystery episode?

(Right)
25 Whose memorial is
    this?
26 When did the person
    die?
27 Which Common lies
    just to the south east?
28 Between which two
    Dartmoor tors does it
    stand?
29 Which beauty spot is
    nearby at the bottom
    of the hill named after
    it?
30 What are the two near-
    est Dartmoor pubs, as
    the crow flies, to this
    cross?

31 Which river is this?
32 Which 'Steps' are just behind the photographer?
33 Which 'spooky' tor sits on the right hand shoulder of the picture?
34 How many 'Stones' are just beyond that tor?
35 In which direction does this river flow for the next mile or so?
36 Which stream joins this river just behind the point where this picture was taken?

37 Who was on the throne of England when this reservoir was built?
38 Which river has been dammed here?
39 Which leat now pours its waters into the reservoir?
40 Which tor is in the right background?
41 Which leat was submerged when the reservoir started to fill up?
42 When did a member of the Elford family hide in a 'cave', on the hill above the valley,
    when being hunted?

43 At which tor, well worth crossing any road for, is this picture taken?
44 Which river runs below it?
45 Which letterbox, sometimes referred to as 'the Cranmere of the Southern Moor' is located not far from the head of this river?
46 What is the name of the next road bridge downstream?
47 What substance is mined and quarried in large amounts in this area?
48 The tor in the picture is located on the side of a high ridge. What is it called?

49 In which moorland settlement would you find this distinct landmark?
50 What is the local nickname for it?
51 What two large hills rise above the town?
52 What word, associated with the past tin industry, always features on the town's name signs?
53 What is the nearest Dartmoor reservoir to this place?
54 What is the source for the water which fills the local swimming pool?

(Right)
55 In which village would you find this pub?
56 What is the name of the pub?
57 Who was the famous long-serving landlady?
58 Which long-distance footpath passes through this village?
59 What is the name of the other pub in the village?
60 Which National Trust property is close to the village?

(Left)
61 In which quarter of which century did this railway open?
62 What is the family name associated with the quarries and railway?
63 The family home, near a country park of the same name, was also the name of a short canal associated with them. What was the word common to all three?
64 What type of stone was used for the railway lines?
65 What was carried along this railway?
66 Which large wood did the railway pass through on leaving Haytor Down?

(Right)
67 Which Dartmoor village is this?
68 Which 'Day' is celebrated in style in the village orchard?
69 What is the village pub called?
70 What was the terminus for the branch line that went up the valley?
71 Which river flows through this lovely village?
72 What was the title of Cecil Torr's book based on life, observations and travels from a property in this village?

(Left)
73 Which castle is to the left of the pub?
74 What is the pub called?
75 Which National Trust tourist attraction is nearby?
76 Which river runs through it?
77 Which ancient trackway ends at the church here?
78 What is unusual about an epitaph near the entrance to the church?

(Right)
79 What is the name of this hamlet?
80 What is/was the main Dartmoor industry in this area?
81 Which river flows through this valley?
82 What is the name of the pub?
83 William Duke (a name not a title) once owned the quarry here. What title was bestowed on his son who was a judge and cabinet minister?

84 In which decade was the current road bridge over the river built to replace the former one?
(Below)
85 This Dartmoor village green has plenty of trees, many planted for special royal occasions. Which village is it?
86 Nearby is a large, golfing hotel, once owned by the railways but no longer. What is its present name?
87 Which tor looks down from on high at this village?
88 What is the village pub called?
89 What granite construction, on the edge of the green, stands opposite the pub?
90 Which river flows past this village?

(Below)
91 This view, taken on Northern Dartmoor, looks down the valley of a small stream. What is it called?
92 What 'Steps' are at the confluence of a river and this stream down the slope from where the photo is taken?
93 Which river does this tributary stream join?
94 Which 'Wall' climbs the distant hillside?
95 On which of the Dartmoor firing ranges is this scene?
96 Which month of the year is there traditionally no firing here?

And finally, in this section:
97 Which of these 16 pictures shows Prestonbury?
98 Which picture was taken the closest to Okehampton?
99 With which picture was the Plymouth Corporation associated?
100 Which picture, had it been taken early in the twentieth century, would have had a row of cottages in it?

26. Dartmoor's Myths, Legends, Folklore and Ghosts
1 What colour clothes do pixies supposedly wear?
2 Which wicked witch has a tor named after her?
3 Which Dartmoor settlement had a famous 'Dancing Tree'?
4 In which town would you find Cutty Dyer?
5 How many 'Maidens' were turned to stone on Belstone Common?
6 Which pool calls out the name of the next person to die, from the parish of Walkhampton, on Midsummer's Night?
7 Which family saw many of its members die after a visitation from a white bird?
8 Which 'Rock' was constructed by three maidens before breakfast?
9 In which village would you find the Oxenham Arms?
10 Which river 'claims a heart' each year, it's said?

11 Which most evil of men, buried at Buckfastleigh church, was said to be the inspiration for the *Hound of the Baskervilles*?

12 Which 'Lady' is condemned to ride to Okehampton Castle every night in a ghostly coach constructed from the bones of the four husbands she is 'alleged' to have murdered?

See Question 13

13 What hirsute happening occurs between Postbridge and Cherry Brook Bridge?

14 What phantom creatures are often just visible in the mist on Merripit Hill?

15 Who was the giant turned to stone on Hayne Down?

16 Which poor moorland lad, returning home across the moor from a courting session with his beloved, had the misfortune to be spotted by the pixies who made him dance until the sun came up? The experience was so traumatic that he never ventured out across the moor to see her again. (Sounds like a dodgy excuse to me!)

17 What was the name of the Hunter who died in a blizzard after trying to shelter in the carcass of his dead horse?

18 The ghost of David Davies, a man who spent most of his lifetime banged up in Dartmoor Prison, has often been seen on the moor. Why is his ghost always seen outside the prison walls?

19 When do the 'Nine Maidens' dance?

20 Who was the wife of the eccentric vicar who dedicated stones in and beside the River Cowsic to favourite poets, having lines of their work engraved on them?

21 Which Dartmoor Pool is bottomless, or so it is said?

22 Where would you find Benji?

23 In which Cleave will you find Roman ghosts?

24 What food was offered to Bishop Branscombe?

25 Which town is haunted by the 9.15 p.m. ghost?

27. The Tom Cobley Walk

This map first appeared in Terry Bound's excellent book *The Great Walks of Dartmoor*. It was used to illustrate a walk called 'Tom Cobley's Walk' based on a possible route taken in the famous song 'Widecombe Fair'. If you recall, a number of men went to Widecombe, became somewhat drunk and climbed aboard the unfortunate Grey Mare.

1 Who were the characters featured in the song?
2 What is the name of the village (S), about 4 km to the north of Whiddon Down, where this walk commenced?
3 Which village, with the fine church of St Mary the Virgin, is T on the map?
4 Which village (G) has an ancient castle?
5 What is the stannary town at C?
6 Which two rivers join just to the west of this stannary town at J?
7 Which reservoir (M) is located on the more southerly of these two rivers?
8 Which pub (W) is located at King's Oven?
9 What is the area known as where the Tom Cobley Walk passes from Frenchbeer to King's Oven?
10 Which tor is the triangle beside Grimspound?
11 On the ridge beyond this tor are several boundary stones marked 'DS'. What do the letters stand for?
12 What was mined between King's Oven and Grimspound?
13 Which creatures link Spreyton, Warren House and Widecombe?
14 What is an older name for King's Oven?
15 Which ancient route does this walk overlap in places?

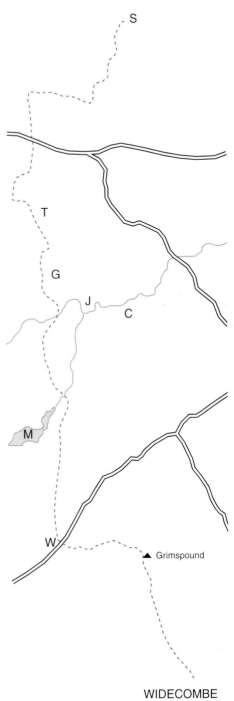

WIDECOMBE

28. The North/South Walk

For many years hundreds of walkers gamely slogged their way along the North/South Walk, a transmoor route. Their task was made somewhat easier by having the luxury of a starting point some six miles into the moor and at one of Dartmoor's highest points. This sketch map, which has been amended, is again taken from Terry Bound's *Great Walks of Dartmoor*.

1 The map shows that the walk started from 'Okement Bunker' but how was it denoted in letters and numbers, there being many of these bunkers or 'Splinter Proofs' in that area?
2 Which legendary 'pool' lies just about a mile to the south of it?
3 Which tor, the first triangle heading southwards, lies in the heart of the wilderness?
4 Which fiendish tor is the next triangle to the south?
5 Which village is marked with a circle to the south west of Two Bridges?
6 Whose Tomb lies along the route?
7 Which 'pool' is to the south of this?
8 To whom is it a memorial?
9 On which river is Harford located?
10 At which dormitory town does this walk end, as shown by the lower circle?
11 Which tramway does this route follow for several of the last miles?
12 The route passes close to two famous woods of stunted oak trees, Wistman's Wood is one but what is the other?
13 How many 'Barrows' are passed, in a single place name on Ugborough Moor?
14 Which appropriately named tor is located close to the intersection of the North/South route and the Lich Way?
15 Which river, one which was once earmarked for a reservoir, is crossed just to the north of the 'Tomb' on this map?

OKEHAMPTON

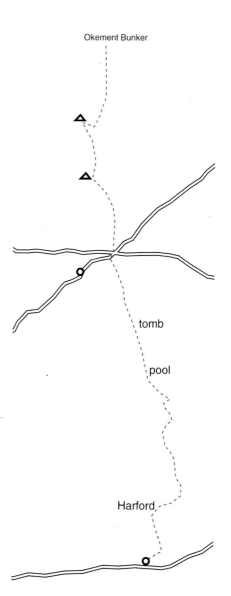

Okement Bunker

tomb

pool

Harford

29. The Abbots' Way

The Abbots' Way is a famous route that linked abbeys on different edges of the moor. But what do you know about it?

1. Which three abbeys have been connected with paths across the moor?
2. From which abbey have the Abbots' Way organised walks generally set off?
3. When travelling westwards from Cross Furzes which stream is first crossed?
4. Which reservoir is skirted just on the southern side of Dean Moor?
5. (Right) Which weather-beaten cross takes its name from the locality and is close to the confluence of the Western Wella Brook and River Avon?
6. This cross was one of four, believed to have been erected in 1557 by a man who was the King's Commissioner and also Secretary of State to four Tudor Sovereigns. Who was this man, whose name features in a nearby feature?
7. Who wrote a guide book to the Abbot's Way in 1935?
8. On the map, which named ford is just to the west of this cross?
9. What is the alternative name for Nun's Cross?
10. What is the alternative, and more contemporary, name for Beckamoor Cross?

30. A Pot Pourri

1. Which Welsh mountain name is found close to the head of the Western Wella Brook?
2. What is the name of the rocks on Ugborough Beacon?
3. Which stream runs along Blatchford Bottom?
4. Which river do Red Lake and Dry Lake fall into?
5. What do Collard Tor, Whitehill Tor, Blackalder Tor and Crownhill Tor have in common?
6. (Right) Which leat drops down Raddick Hill?
7. Which 'Down', taking its name from a hamlet, acts as a divide between the Holy Brook and the River Mardle?
8. What is the only named hill on the OS map between Higher Cherry Brook Bridge and Lower Cherry Brook Bridge?

See Question 6

9. What is Rippator's alternative name, at least according to the map?
10. What do Hemstone Rocks, Tom's Hill and Sandeman Bridge have in common, today?

11 Which tor lies between Dunstone Down and Bittleford Down?

12 Which wood envelops Kraps Ring?

13 Which river does Bellever Bridge span?

14 Which river rises at Blue Jug?

15 (Right) On which down is Bowerman's Nose?

16 Beside which river would you find Kit Rocks, Broad Marsh and Roundy Park?

(Above) See Question 15

(Below) See Question 20

17 What is the closest tor to Limsboro Cairn?

18 What was the approximate weight, in pounds, of an ingot of tin?

19 How many ingots could be carried by a pack horse?

20 (Right) What was the nickname of the hermit, Frederick William Symes, who spent many years at Huntingdon Warren close to the scene in the picture?

21 What was a 'vooga' used for in medieval times on the moors?

22 Beside which river would you find the Phillips Leat?

23 What is a 'creep' on Dartmoor?

24 What was the earlier name for a dolmen?

25 What was the name of the route forged through the

peat fen from the Upper East Dart to the Upper Tavy area?

26 What name connects a Bishop of Exeter, a writer called Eden and a peat-cutter called Frank?

27 In which Dartmoor churchyard is the famous Dartmoor writer Eric Hemery, who died in 1986, buried?

28 The Bourchiers carried the title the Earls of Bath. Their symbol was the Bourchier Knot only found in two Devon churches. One is Haccombe, near Newton Abbot, but where is the other?

29 In 1995 a stone was carved on Holne Moor to the memory of a man who was held in the highest esteem by those who knew him, he having been the Reeve of Holne Moor for thirty years. The stone, sited near Horse Ford on the O Brook, bears the H for Holne and his initials 'AB' but what was his name?

30 What is another name for 'the Coronet' found in the East Okement valley?

31. Dartmoor's Churches and Chapels

1 To which saint is the church on Brentor dedicated?
2 Where did the Keble-Martin brothers set up a chapel?
3 Where was Squire Cabell buried?
4 St Mary's is found on a hill above the Walkham valley, just up the hill from Ward Bridge. What is the name of the hamlet in which this lovely church is located?
5 Which famous writer, often associated with North Devon, was born in the vicarage at Holne?
6 In which place's church is there a memorial to George Parker Bidder, a character who became famous as 'The Calculating Boy' on account of his extraordinary mathematical skills? Outside the church was a famous tree where a small dance floor, of sorts, was erected in the upper branches.
7 Where would you find a church dedicated to the seventh century Welsh saint, Winifred? The rocks on the hill above the church take their name from the village below and a former vicar fell out with some of the pall bearers when he refused to let funeral processions walk three times around a cross before entering the church.
8 This church lies in a small hamlet where, in the Queen's Jubilee year of 1977, they inscribed a stone to that effect. This church of St John the Baptist lies high up on the shoulder of the hill above the Webburn Valley. What is the name of the hamlet?
9 The Drewes lie buried here, Lutyens having designed the tomb. Which village is this?
10 This church of Holy Trinity stands high above the North Teign river, close to a castle, now a private property but still with a small square keep. Which small village is this?

32. Ten Tors?

Can you name the ten/eleven tors which lie on the boundary line of the Forest of Dartmoor? If you did the Perambulation, as described in Terry Bound's *Great Walks of Dartmoor,* these are the granite piles you would pass.

33. H is for Walkham?

The River Walkham has many places, more than twenty, along it which begin with the letter 'H', ALL being below Merrivale Bridge. Without looking at the 1:25 000 map, how many can

you name from within a kilometre or so either side of the river? You are allowed repeats for 'Farms' and 'Bridges' and so on.

34. When is a Lake Not a Lake?

Name the 'Lakes' which join the Erme between Erme Head and Ivybridge.

35. At the Sourton Crossroads

Sourton Cross has four faces, each bearing a letter, these being H, O, L, and T. What does each letter represent?

36. Go North West Young Man!

The Lich Way crosses four rivers between Cherry Brook and Lydford. What are they?

37. Animal Crackers South

Below is another base map from Terry Bound's *Great Walks of Dartmoor*. (See also page 15.)

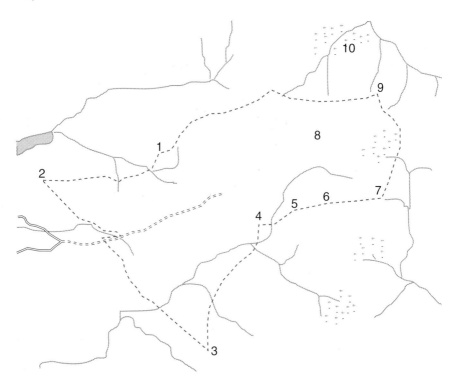

Match the ten numbers on the map with the 'animal' names that are in this list: Sheeps Tor, Hartor Tor, Great Gnats' Head, Hen Tor, Crane Hill, Fox Tor, Foxtor Mires, Cuckoo Rock, Calveslake Tor and Ducks' Pool.

38. Wheels Within Wheals

Many of the mines or 'wheals' in on and around the moor had boys' or girls' names. How many can you name?

39. Even 'Moor' Names

1 Tor for a rabbit or a deer? (3)
2 So light this tor might just float away! (7)
3 A quarry that is not clear to see? (9)
4 Quarries with a lump? (8)
5 Highest tor but not really! (3)
6 Refreshments at Poundsgate? (9, 3)
7 Not a nice place to hang about! (6, 4)
8 Spoilt child's tor (4)
9 Charles Dickens' literary house? (5, 5)
10 Not the Boiling North Cross! (4, 4, 5)
11 Cinderella's Steps? (6)
12 Raining hard? (10, 6)
13 Argumentative tor? (3)
14 Apart from a couple of tablets, what God gave to Moses (3, 12)
15 Tom and Sally's end product of a Dartmoor day (5, 4, 3)
16 A river to squeeze? (5)
17 A good golfing tor? (5, 5)
18 Cuckoo and Corringdon? (5)
19 Cowflop, Deadman's and Doe Tor (7)
20 The Doctor's Drive? (8)

See Question 6

40. Twenty Toughies

More obscure clues to moorland places:

1 Wet tree connection? (5, 3, 6)
2 Ensconced judges tor (5)
3 A most painful complaint in the Erme Valley (6, 5)
4 Drainage Tor? (6)
5 Transplant for a deer? (4, 3)
6 Going better than BP! (5, 3)
7 What BT and other phone companies might appreciate (8, 4)
8 Walkham's scary crossing place (11)

See Question 5

9   Treasure? (5, 2, 4)
10 Fishy tor on a golf course (4)
11 Broken bones fixed but where did the surgeon begin? (7, 4)
12 Apartment rock? (4, 3)
13 First Aid Outcrop (5, 3)
14 A hill where you shouldn't sit or lie down (7)
15 She's got six balls, but no runs! (6, 4)
16 Lynne Perry, Colin Welland and Brian Glover featured in this 1969 film (3)
17 Look out for this Somerset coastal elevation (7, 4)
18 This former dwelling figures (6, 5)
19 Game hill? (8)
20 Angela on the moor? (6, 3)

41. The Lich Way

The Lich Way, otherwise known as the Way of the Dead, was a route across open moorland used when coffins had to be taken to the parish church of Lydford, on the western side of Dartmoor, to be buried.

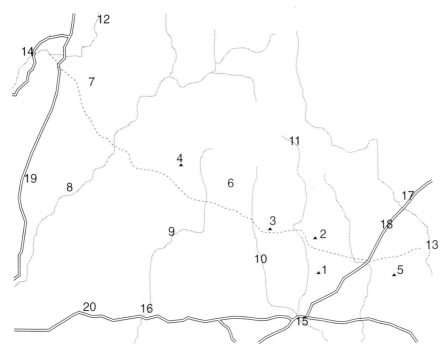

Can you name:
The tors (1–5)
The hills (6–7)
The rivers/streams (8–12)
The hamlets and villages (13–17)
The road classification/numbers for three roads (18–20)

42. Wise about Widecombe?

This moorland village is one of the most visited and famous places in Devon but how much do you know about it? *Widecombe – A Visitors' Guide* will tell you much more about this famous place.

1　How many travelled to Widecombe in the famous folk song? (Think carefully about this!)
2　Who lent the horse?
3　Which famous preservationist designed the present village sign?
4　What is the name of the village green?

5　What are the village's two pubs called?
6　What item of 'Uncle Tom's' furniture is housed in the Glebe House?
7　Who has two names on her gravestone, the other being her birth name Olive Katharine Parr?
8　Which logan stone, of immense proportions, lies on private land behind the pub in the nearby hamlet of Venton?
9　What do Edward Dunn, Simon Northmore and Peter Hicks have in common?
10　What happened in the village on 21 October 1638?

43. Primed about Princetown?

Princetown is the highest 'town' in Devon and therefore the wettest and coldest but it has a history.

1　For which nationality of person was the prisoner of war depot built?
2　Which nationality joined them in 1812?
3　What Latin phrase appears above the entrance to the prison?
4　Who built Conchies Road?
5　Which Dartmoor tor is portrayed, at regularly spaced intervals, in the public conveniences at Princetown?
6　What was the name of the High Dartmoor Interpretation Centre in the days when it was a hotel?

7   What is the name of the track that leads southwards out of Princetown towards South
    Hessary Tor?
8   Which bridge lies on the road between Princetown and Two Bridges?
9   What is the name of the lane that runs southwards from Princetown towards the
    Whiteworks?
10 What is the name of the hole in a cell door used by warders to see in?

44. Clued-up on Chagford?

Chagford is a Stannary Town which served the north-eastern quadrant of Dartmoor. These
questions will be really easy if you've read *The Great Little Chagford Book*!

1   Which shop houses a 'museum' featuring many bits and bobs which reflect the town's
    past?
2   Which other well-known Ironmonger family firm has been trading in the Square since
    1898?
3   Which Chagford pub, often garlanded in fantastic flowers, is named after a famous
    Devonshire general?
4   The railways never reached Chagford despite plans to link it to the network so what was
    the nearest railway town?
5   What is the name of Chagford's twin town, in the area known as Calvados, in Normandy?
6   Who was shot dead on her wedding day on 11 October 1641?

7 Whose memorial, a giant granite monolith, was hauled through Chagford in 1904 on its way to its final resting place at Pirbright? His nickname was 'Bula Matari', meaning 'the rock breaker'.

8 Who stayed at the Easton Court near Chagford in 1944 and wrote *Brideshead Revisited*?

9 What name is given to both a hilltop tower and a set of fording steps across the Teign?

10 What was the name of Chagford's former 'regal' cinema?

45. OK on Okehampton?

Okehampton sits on the northern boundary of the national park. There is a fine trilogy of books written by Mike and Hilary Wreford which show, in tremendous graphic detail, what the town has looked like down the years.

1 Which two rivers meet here?
2 What is the name of the town's cinema?
3 What is the town's principal park called?
4 What suffix follows the name 'Okehampton' in the town's soccer team?
5 In which hotel have the Emperor of Ethiopia (Haile Selassie), William Pitt the Elder and Ian Botham all stayed?
6 What game is played east of Estrayer Park just outside the town?
7 What surface reservoir is closest to Okehampton?
8 What is the name of the small village, a few miles to the north of Okehampton, where 'Okehampton Aerodrome' was located?
9 Which road now by-passes the town?
10 What is the name of the viaduct that spans the East Okement just outside the town?

46. Dartmoor Books from Long Ago

Who wrote these novels from the past? (some of which are mega-obscure but all of which prominently featured Dartmoor).

1	The Grey Room	2	Lethbridge of the Moor
3	To Call Her Mine	4	Pages of Peace
5	My Lady of the Moor	6	Christowell
7	The Wingless Victory	8	The Mallorys
9	The Fourth Dimensions	10	A Pixy in Petticoats
11	The French Prisoner	12	Love the Intruder
13	John Herring	14	Joanna and His Reverence
15	Lady Mary of Tavistock	16	Romances of the West
17	Drake's Drum	18	The Jingle Driver
19	The Ponson Case	20	The Queen of the Moor
21	Mr Lyndon at Liberty	22	The Iron Stair
23	Lucky Mr Loder	24	The Creggan Peerage
25	The Lifting of the Shadow	26	Room 13
27	Morwenna of the Green Gown	28	George Goring's Daughters
29	The Thing at Their Heels	30	The Statue

47. Odd Man Out

Pick the one that you think is the odd one out and give the reason.

1 Wistman's Wood, Fernworthy Forest, Piles Copse, Black Tor Copse
2 Moretonhampstead, Ashburton, Bovey Tracey, Okehampton, Princetown, Lydford, Buckfastleigh, Chagford
3 Yes Tor, Devil's Tor, Crow Tor, Staple Tors, Combestone Tor, Littaford Tors, Dinger Tor, Great Links Tor, Arms Tor
4 Meavy, Horrabridge, Walkhampton, Merrivale
5 Dart, Teign, Erme, Taw, Avon, Yealm
6 Bowerman, Vixana, Tyrwhitt, Cutty Dyer, Will O'the Wisp
7 Fingle Bridge, Cadover Bridge, Shaugh Bridge, Laira Bridge, Plym Bridge
8 Walkhampton, Princetown, Sheepstor, Horrabridge, Christow, Dunsford, Wonson, Postbridge, Merrivale, North Bovey
9 Buckfastleigh, Ashburton, Tavistock, Lydford, Chagford
10 Queen Victoria, William Crossing, Anthony Cave-Penney, the Crew of the Handley Page Hampden 'S' X3054, Nigel Duncan Ratcliff Hunter, Sir Walter Raleigh

48. Timber!

Can you see the woods for the missing letters?

Here is a list of various woods, plantations and forests within the National Park, some are well-known but with others you might just be barking up the wrong tree! Please use a map if you have difficulty in 'logging' the right answers.

1 B – – – – – – – (near Postbridge)
2 F– – – – – – – – – (a few miles west of Chagford)
3 S– – – – – Wood (near Sticklepath)
4 S– – – – – – – D– – – (near Warren House)
5 Y– – – – – Wood (access by permit)
6 H– – – – – – Wood (near Becky Falls)
7 S– – – – – – Wood (near Lustleigh)
8 L– – – – – – Plantation (near Manaton)
9 D– – – – – – Wood (near Cornwood)
10 R– – – – – – Plantation (near Burrator)

11 P– – – – – – Wood (near Ivybridge)
12 H– – – – – D– – – C– – – – (near Cornwood)
13 P– – – – – – Wood
14 B– – – – – – – Wood (near Meavy)
15 O– – – – – – – – Plantation (near Yelverton)
16 S– – – – – – – – – – Wood (near Grenofen)
17 O– – – – – – – – Wood (between Shipley and South Brent)
18 C– – – – – – – – – – Wood (near South Brent)
19 B– – – – – – – Wood (in the Walkham valley)
20 S– – – – – P– – – Plantation (near Dartmeet)

49. Dartmoor's Railroads – or Something along Those Lines!

1 What was carried along the Omen Beam Tramroad in the mid 1840s?
2 What was this turned into?
3 In which village or town did this happen?
4 What did the premises, where this occurred, become a few years later?
5 This line started on the open moor at a point on the OS map stated as Greena Ball but what other name has been given to this location?
6 In connection with the Omen Beam Tramroad what might the letters BPNC represent?
7 What was the main use of the Red Lake Railway, going into the heart of southern Dartmoor?
8 Which Dartmoor writer was engaged as the civil engineer for the Red Lake Railway?
9 What 'Lake', other than Red Lake, was also excavated along this route?
10 In which decade did this venture finish for good, the lines being taken up?
11 Which beautiful Dartmoor valley runs almost parallel just to the west of the Red Lake Railway?
12 How were clays transported here?
13 With which long distance (if you call 17 miles long) path, through the Teignbridge district, is the Haytor Granite Tramway associated?
14 What material was used for the railway lines?

15 From which quarry, shown here, did "Nineteen stout horses, it was known…drew the stone"?

16 How did the men, who escorted the stone-carrying wagons, know how far they would have travelled at regular intervals?

17 With which canal did the Haytor Granite Tramway link?

18 Stover House, near Stover Countryside Park, became the home of the Templers. What is Stover House today?

19 Who acquired both the canal and the tramway in the late 1820s?

20 Who wrote the book *The Templer Way*?

21 Which television science-fiction character filmed along this tramway?

22 Through the edge of which Nature Reserve does the tramway pass?

23 Where was the junction, shown here, where the line from Princetown met the line from Plympton to Tavistock South?

24 Which famous railway engineer was engaged, after the untimely death of the commissioned engineer, to complete the railroad, for the South Devon & Tavistock Railway Company, from Plympton to Tavistock?

25 What was the name of the viaduct which spanned the Walkham along this route?

26 Which 'precious-sounding' mine, which had various names, was found in the shadow of this impressive viaduct?

27 Which 'ornithological' viaduct stood above Bedford Bridge on this same line?

28 In which year did the Princetown–Yelverton branch line close?

29 What were the four stops for passengers between Yelverton and Princetown?

30 Which of these had a warning about adders on the platform?

31 The topography of the land dictated that this line took some enormous curves around the contours, one of the biggest being the loop out around King's Tor. What large granite quarries were almost encircled by this great sweep?

32 Which Dartmoor railway station was used in the filming of the 1931 version of *Hound of the Baskervilles* and once had a memorial to the station cat?

33 What was the original terminus on the line that runs from Totnes to Buckfastleigh with steam trains today?

34 In which former railway station, shown here, do Thompson's have their lorry depot?

35 At which station were there two lines, the GWR and the SR running through?

36 Add the number of tunnels, to the number of viaducts, found along the Newton Abbot–Moretonhampstead line and what is your total?

37 What now runs along part of the trackbed of the former line between Ashburton and Buckfastleigh?

38 The station, shown here, was on the Teign Valley line, in the centre of an important mining and quarrying area. Which station is it?

39 Where did the Teign Valley link with the Newton Abbot to Moretonhampstead branch?

40 As the crow flies, what was the nearest passenger station to Cranmere Pool?

50. Picture Postcard Posers

Here you have another chance to score the perfect 100 per cent with 20 pictures each with five questions about them. We are now well into the book and if you have worked through it systematically you will have realised that many questions crop up again and again, so you should have learnt some of the answers by now, if you didn't know them at first.

1 Which town is this?

2 What does it have instead of a Mayor?

3 A Devonshire dialect expert, whose dulcet tones are frequently heard on local radio lives here. Who is he?

4 What was the nickname of the local train which ran to Totnes?

5 On the town's coat of arms there are a sun and a moon but what do they represent?

(Right)

6 Which village is this?

7 The picture shows the village post office but what was it before?

8 Which giant hill lies just to the south east and once was, wrongly, believed to be the highest hill in Devon?

9 Which river runs between this village and this 'gert' hill?

10 Which cleave lies between the village and Sticklepath?

(Right)

11 What is this well-known waterfall?

12 What is the name of the stream that tumbles down over these rocks?

13 Of which river is this a tributary?

14 These falls look more spectacular after heavy rain and did so after South Devon was hit by a hurricane on August Bank Holiday of 1986. What was the hurricane called?

15 What water-loving creature was adopted as the trade mark of this tourist attraction?

(Above)

16 What is the name of this tor which has a name shared by many others on Dartmoor?

17 What is the name of the 'Drive' which ends a short distance away?

18 What is the nearest pub?

19 Which river flows at the base of the hill on which this tor is located?

20 Which reservoir lies on the opposite side of this valley?

(Below)
21 This is taken close to a beauty spot favoured by Plymothians. Where is it?
22 Which river flows through here?
23 What is the next road bridge downstream?
24 Which precipitous, cliff-like rock lies on the north bank about half a mile downstream from here?
25 On which nearby tor is Red Quarry found?

(Right)
26 In which village would you find this bridge?
27 Which river does it span?
28 What is the fishy name of the pub near the bridge?
29 What is the name of the next road bridge upstream?
30 Which 'Diary', from about 1902, was inspired by the countryside in and around this bridge?

(Below)
31 Which 'castle' is this?
32 What is the pub called beside it?
33 What purpose did the 'castle' have for the Stannaries?
34 What was the status of Richard Strode who spent about a year here, in none too luxurious circumstances?
35 Which river flows nearby?

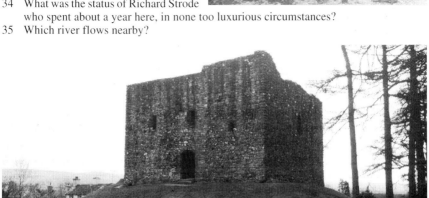

(Below)
36 Which well-detached Dartmoor pub is this?
37 Which animals are depicted above the doorway?
38 What industry was prominent in the vicinity of the pub?
39 Which large forest appears at the back of this picture?
40 What is the strangely named hill within this plantation which is derived from a story
where a father challenges a potential son-in-law to carry a heavy burden quite a distance?

(Right)
41 What is the name of the hill?
42 What is flowing down the hillside?
43 In which century was it built?
44 Into which reservoir are most of these waters now discharged?
45 Which river does the launder (water chute) carry this flow of water over?

(Below)
46 Either it's a drought or somebody's pulled the plug on this Dartmoor reservoir but which one?
47 Which river has been dammed to create the reservoir? (When it's there!)
48 What is the name of the double stone circle close to where this river rises?
49 Which area does it supply with water?
50 On what, near the reservoir, is carved "Jesus said 'I am the way, the truth and the light'"?

(Right)

51 Which river is flowing in this waterfall about two miles above Postbridge?

52 What is the name of the 'Pass' just to the north west of here?

53 On the back of which book cover is this picture featured?

54 Which appropriately-named 'Ring' lies on the south east side of Broad Down, farther downstream?

55 If you walked north-east from here, which wood would be reached in about two miles?

(Below)

56 What is the name of this old mine?

57 What is the name given to the line of roadside stones shown in the picture?

58 What is the name of this extensive down?

59 Which Tavistock-centred BBC drama, from 1994/95 shot some sequences in this immediate area?

60 Which Dartmoor firing range lies to the north-east?

(Above)

61 Whose roadside grave is this?

62 How did that person die?

63 Why did the person do this?

64 Who wrote a short story, based on this episode, called *The Apple Tree* which was made into a feature film called *Summer Story*?

65 What is the name of the low down, opposite this grave, on the eastern side of the road?

(Right)

66 This is the grave of one of Dartmoor's most famous writers, famous for his 'Guide', who died in 1928. Who was he?

67 Which Dartmoor letterbox is dedicated to his memory?

68 Where was he born?

69 Where did his family own a mill?

70 In which newspaper did his *Hundred Years on Dartmoor* and *Gems in a Granite Setting* first appear?

(Below)

71 This former filling station took its name from the tor on the hill. What is that tor?

72 What has this filling station now become?

73 What is the name of the nearby hamlet which includes a pub called the Rock Inn?

74 Which popular Dartmoor writer lived here until he died?

75 Which American comedian, with a high-pitched voice, filmed a comedy sketch on the forecourt of this filling station? Gabrielle Drake was playing his screen wife.

(Below)

76 Pre-by-pass but eerily devoid of traffic, where is this once traffic-choked place?

77 Which long distance walking cricketer stopped at the White Hart here on one of his great walks?

78 Which film, based on a Cornish story written by Daphne du Maurier, was filmed close to this town, because Dartmoor was preferred to Bodmin Moor as a backcloth?

79 What are the names of the three military firing ranges?

80 What is the name of the well, by the side of the road leading to the army camp, whose waters are purported to be good for eye disorders?

(Right)
81 What is the name of this granite construction?
82 What is the name for this type of structure?
83 When did three unmarried ladies build this, according to the story?
84 Which village lies just over two miles to the east of this feature?
85 Which village lies about two miles to the south of it?

(Left)
86 What is the name of this small town with a long place name?
87 What was supposedly painted on the town's gasometer to encourage enemy bombers to go elsewhere during the Second World War?
88 What arrived in the town in 1866, but departed in 1959?

89 This was the birthplace of a lad called George Parker Bidder (1806–1878) who was a Mathematical genius achieving considerable fame for his skills. What was his related nickname?
90 Where in South Devon was this Victorian 'whizz-kid' buried?

(Above)
91 Which Dartmoor reservoir is this?
92 On which river does it stand?
93 What was extracted here for a glassworks to be established in the 1880s?
94 What colour were most of the bottles which were manufactured here for holding minerals or medicines?
95 Which MP opened this reservoir in 1972?

(Left)
96 In which gorge would you find this waterfall?
97 What is the name of the waterfall?
98 Who manages this tourist attraction?
99 Who has a Cauldron here?
100 What was the name of the gang of red-haired horse thieves who lived in holes in the ground here long ago?

51. Ten Bridges, not Two Bridges!

1 What is an alternative name for Bedford Bridge, which spans the Walkham?
2 Which stone bridge lies between Bedford Bridge and the Walkham's confluence with the Tavy?
3 At which bridge does the B3357 apparently end?
4 Which river flows under Huccaby Bridge?
5 What is the first small road bridge the infant Harbourne passes under?
6 Which river is spanned by Spara Bridge?
7 Which river passes under Drakeford Bridge?
8 What is the next road bridge downstream from Postbridge?
9 There are two Harford Bridges on Dartmoor, one spans the Erme but which river does the other one cross?
10 What is the name of the bridge, near Chagford, spanning the Blackaton Brook, which shares a name with a famous soccer stadium?

52. 'Deleted' Leats

Fill in the 'deleted' letters of these Leats:

1 – – –o–p– –t
2 G– – –s– –n– & – –rt– –d–e
3 –ra– –'–
4 –o–n– M– – –
5 W–e– – –m– –
6 D– –o– –h– –l –ri– –d–h– –
7 B– – – – – – – and – – –i– –r M– – –
8 H– – – – ri– – –
9 G– –l– –g–
10 –y– –s– –r–o– M– – –

53. Joined in Aquatic Matrimony?

Which two rivers meet at each of the following places?

1 Double Waters
2 Lizwell Meet
3 Okehampton
4 Dartmeet
5 Buckland Bridge
6 Shaugh Bridge
7 Two Bridges
8 Leigh Bridge
9 Bere Ferrers
10 Buckfastleigh

54. Beating the Bounds ... or Being Beaten by Them?

Opposite is a map of Dartmoor with a series of numbers and letters to represent all the different parishes on and around the moor. If you look closely you will see that there are some 46 parishes shown here. All you have to do is name them, initial letters being given to make your task that much easier.

1	A	2	B	3	B		
4	B	5	B	6	B & S		
7	BM	8	BM	9	B		
10	BT	11	B	12	C		
13	C	14	C	15	D		
16	D	17	DP	18	G		
19	H	20	H	21	H		
22	H	23	I	24	I		
25	L	26	L	27	M		
28	M	29	M	30	MT		
31	NB	32	O	33	P		
34	PT	35	S	36	S		
37	SB	38	SP	39	SS		
40	ST	41	T	42	T		
43	U	44	W	45	W		
46	W						

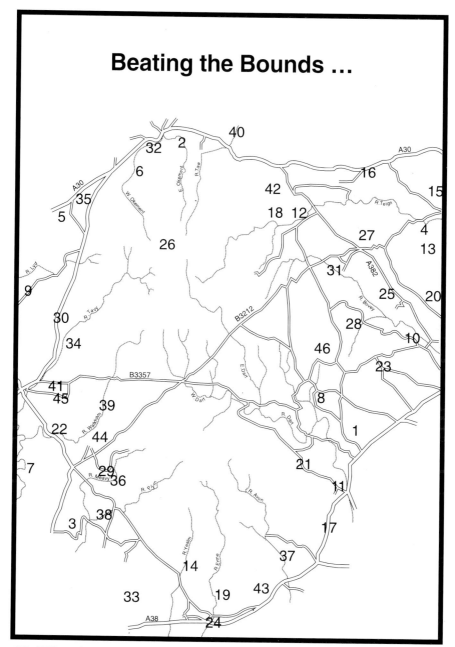

Beating the Bounds …

55. When is a Tor Not a Tor?

William Crossing, in his book *Amid Devonia's Alps*, listed 12 outcrops which he considered to be "Rock Piles on Dartmoor not reckoned as Tors". Can you name them?

56. Dartmoor Knows No Bounds?

1. What do the letters EPB represent on the bound stones on the Ashburton/Buckland parish boundary?

2. What is unusual, perhaps even surprising, about the granite used for a series of five boundary markers, by the Dartmoor Preservation Association, around Sharpitor?

3. What do the letters WV stand for on a bound stone above the mine which now has more names than miners?

4. There are four bound stones along the southern side of Soussons Wood but what letters do they bear and what is this an abbreviation for?

See Question 1

5. What do the letters BB stand for on Broad Rock?

6. Who, in the mid nineteenth century, is attributed with a number of 'stones' that include 'Prince Albert' and 'Victoria' (and the one in the picture)?

See Question 6

7. For which reservoir's catchment are there stones marked 'PCWW'?

8. If the letters RD appear like the top half of a fraction with H below on one side of the stone and the letters PUDC on the other which reservoir is nearby?

9. The bridge at Sticklepath bears a stone and the initials of two parishes that meet there but which ones are they?

10. Which 'Nest' boundary stone is located where the Widecombe/Ilsington parish bounds meet those of Ashburton?

57. Even Moor Toughies

1. Other than the unfortunate horse in the Widecombe story, what else on the moor is known as 'The Grey Mare'?

2. Which hill has a memorial to the 1930s Dartmoor writer Jeffrey W. Malim of St Marychurch?

3. Where would you find the letters 'MM' on a memorial to a little girl?

4. Which comedy duo made a silent film at Parke, now the HQ of the Dartmoor National Park?

5. What was that silent film called?

6. Which well-known person posed for the cover photograph of her book at Pew Tor?

7. Which Dartmoor-based photographer has made a television series about Exmoor?

8. In which year of the first half of the twentieth century was there a major riot at Dartmoor Prison?

9. Which famous travelling preacher preached on the slope above Sticklepath?

10. In which valley would you find the Slipper Stones?

11. Which creature features on the Belstone Tor letterbox of 1981?

See Question 3

12 (Below) What is the number of the Observation Post on the artillery road at Okement Hill?

13 Which rock with religious overtones stands on Zoar Down?
14 What is its alternative name?
15 What is unusual about a stone wall, at Horndon, which forms part of Tavy Lane running down to a crossing point on the river?
16 Which farm, near Chagford, was the first in the kingdom to have electricity by the turning of a water wheel?
17 Which famous explorer's headstone was taken from near Chagford to Pirbright in Surrey to stand by his grave?
18 In which parish is Deave Lane?
19 What is the only tributary of the Glaze Brook?
20 Where would you find the names Bulteel and Treby etched?
21 What animal connection is found on the north-eastern shoulder of Cosdon?
22 What was the micaceous haematite, mined at the former Kelly Mine, between Bovey and Moreton, known as when used to sprinkle on written documents to dry ink in the past?

23 What is the area, purchased by the DPA in the 1960s, above Hawns and Dendles called?

24 Into what has Elford Town corrupted?

25 What was the name of the war-time airfield on Roborough Down, near Yelverton?

26 What happened to a Typhoon fighter at this airfield in 1944?

27 What is the connection between the Equinoxes, Dartmoor letterboxers and the Forest Inn at Hexworthy?

See Question 23

28 At which pub was part of a Radio 4 programme about Dartmoor letterboxing recorded some years ago?
29 At which pub did Michael Buerk chair a television discussion about the military use of Dartmoor?
30 Why does the line of shops at Yelverton only have one storey when it used to have two?
31 Which Dartmoor pub was the first one to have its own 'Dartmoor Letterbox'?

32　If you followed the following 'Dartmoor Letterbox' clues where would you·end up in Okehampton? "Take the regal step back in time and from a granite post, next to St James' Chapel, go 40 paces on a bearing of 121 degrees to the royal lounge. Then go another 9 paces on a bearing of 321 degrees to locate the box."

33　Near which tor was the long-since disappeared Princetown Rifle Range?

34　Which Dartmoor poet was born at Devonport in 1777, ran away to sea in his teens but returned to compose such celebrated works as the 'Banks of Tamar' (1820)? There is a memorial to him at Shaugh Prior's church but he is buried near Bath.

35　What is a more familiar name for 'Lydford Bridle Path No. 8'?

36　What is an alternative, but fruitier, name for Watern Combe on the northern moor?

37　What was the name of the path used by workers travelling to and fro from work between Peter Tavy and Merrivale?

38　Who is the 'PG' who did a vast number of pen and ink sketch illustrations for William Crossing?

39　(Below) What year do the DPA and the former Princetown passenger railway have in common when it comes to their genesis?

40　In which distinctive rock, on the boundary of Gidleigh parish, is there an etched mark on the inside of its portal?

41　What was, originally, the only intermediate 'stop' on the Yelverton-Princetown branch line?

42　In which year was 'The Great Blizzard'?

43　Whose last book, written in 1926, was a collection of Dartmoor poems entitled *Cranmere Pool*?

44　What was Crossing referring to when he wrote "I would much rather not have seen Dartmoor desecrated by such an innovation!"?

45　Who wrote a poem called 'Ephraim's Pinch'?

46　Below which tor did William Donaghy die in February 1914?

47　Which Dartmoor writer, of the past, had the initials RHW?

48　To what was Rev H. Hugh Breton referring when he mentioned 'Ladle' in his book *The Heart of Dartmoor*?

49　Which gully, part of the Birch Tor Mine, was reputed to contain gold which was protected by a raven?

50　What is the name of the launder that carries the Devonport Leat over the river Meavy at the bottom of Raddick Hill?

51　At which stop on the former Princetown–Yelverton railway line was there a pair of semi-detached residences known as Royal Oak Bungalows?

52　What are 'urts'?

53　At which reservoir was 'Ye Fyshinge Feast' celebrated?

54　Whose 'Pious Memory' was remembered at this 'Feast'?

55　Which two moorland edge abbeys were linked by the Monks' Path?

56　Which is gate is passed through by those who descend from the direction of Crazy Well towards Burrator as Norsworthy Lane begins?

57 Which Dartmoor industry was the brainchild of Plymouth's Alderman Frean in the 1840s?

58 Where did R. D. Wilson, R. L. A. Ellis, C. T. Lyon and R. Brames lose their lives on Dartmoor during the Second World War?

59 Beside which stream was East Hughes Mine?

60 Between which two Downs was Wheal Jewell located?

See Question 57

61 At which former hotel was there a mosaic on the floor that greeted visitors with "Welcome the coming" and sent others off with "Speed the parting guest"?

62 Where were Carpenter, Malim, Ozzard, Franks and Luxton involved in establishing a memorial in 1938?

63 Collectively how were these men known?

64 Which precipitous outcrop probably derived its present name from an Anglo-Saxon phrase that has been interpreted as meaning 'Rock of Doves'?

65 What was the name of the famous bee-keeping monk at Buckfast Abbey who died in the late summer of 1996?

66 What was the late Harry Starkey's pen name for a series of walks featured in the Dartmoor Magazine?

67 Which nineteenth century Dartmoor writer seemed to get terribly confused as to which was the East and West Dart river, often citing the fact that Wistman's Wood was in the East Dart valley?

68 (Below) What was the beautiful Dolly's surname in the Dolly's Cott near Brimpts above Dartmeet?

69 What do the years 1891, 1947 and 1963 have in common?

70 How is Harry Starkey's memory maintained at the school in Chagford?

71 If you walked south-westwards along Vergyland Combe, which river would you join?

72 What is common to Links Tor, Trowlesworthy Tor and Staple Tor?

73 Where would you find Lower and Upper Corner Pools, Shara Pool and Combestone Island Pool?
74 Which isolated Dartmoor Letterbox was established in 1951?
75 Beside which small stream is Grant's Pot?
76 Where was a letterbox established at the request of Mrs Charles Chapman, the wife of the County Commissioner for Scouts, in 1968?
77 Where was a letterbox placed in 1973 by Exeter University students (sponsored by the WMN) to the memory of William Crossing and Robert Burnard?
78 How did Joseph Panton, Patrick Carlin and George Driver meet their fate on Dartmoor in 1853?
79 Beside which river would you have found No 2 'To Virgil' No 16 'To Shakespeare', No 18 'To Milton' and many more etched stones?
80 Which stream rises near the King Wall and flows down to Bridestowe?
81 On which river is Hapstead Ford?
82 Which pathway begins at Michelcombe and leads walkers who follow it to the edge of Fox Tor Mire?
83 What is the name of the low down between the River Lyd and the Dartmoor Inn?
84 What is the real name ascribed to Eden Phillpotts' 'Dunnagoat Cottage' in his novel *The Whirlwind*?
85 Which hill was described by Harry Starkey as having the "...appearance of a pudding turned out of its basin and inverted"?
86 Which cross stands at a point which used to be known as Stascombe's Telling Place?
87 What was counted here in the past?
88 Which two mines, beginning with the letter 'H', were incorporated under the umbrella of 'Hexworthy Mines'?
89 What was the name of the former inn, shown here, located on the junction next to the car park at Hound Tor?
90 What do Babeny, Cholwell and Littlecombe Farms have in common?
91 From the slopes of which tor, it is said, was the stone for the outer layers of Castle Drogo taken?
92 What is another name for Windypost?

See Question 89

93 Which school, close to the road from Two Bridges to Tavistock, had only one headmaster, Mr Stoyle, through its entire life which spanned the years 1915–1936?
94 In which wood, on the Lich Way, was it said that bodies brought straddled over the back of a pack horse were transferred into a coffin for the latter part of the journey?
95 On which firing range is Anthony Stile?
96 Which Princetown-brewed beer won the title for the premium beer in 1995 and 1996?
97 What do Ann, Betsy, Caroline, Dorothy, Eleanor, Emily, Emma, George, Hazel, Katherine, Mary Emma, Rose and Ruth ALL have in common?
98 Which event held at South Zeal celebrated its twenty-first annual occurrence in 1998?
99 Which obscure tor, on private land of Dartmoor Prison, is formed of two piles of granite and appears on William Shillibeer's early nineteenth century map of the area?
100 N. T. Carrington, the Dartmoor Poet, was born in 1777 but what did the 'T' represent in his initials?

58. Clocking On!

Here is that famous clockface from the church at Buckland-in-the-Moor where instead of numerals the words 'My Dear Mother' are spelt out. Here we have removed those letters. Either write down the numbers 1–12 and then put against each number the corresponding letter from the church clock or draw your own clock face and put them in. What could be easier?

59. "Not Another Dartmoor Book?"

As a lover of Dartmoor, you probably have amassed a collection of Dartmoor books and it's amazing how many there are, new ones appearing every season. All you have to do is to complete the titles by working out the missing words which may appear in the title and the missing part of the name of the author. Some are well-known, others more obscure.

1 *Amidst Devonia's (4)*, William (8)
2 *Diary of a Dartmoor (6)*, (5) Barber
3 *(8) of Dartmoor*, (4) Smith
4 *Small talk at (8)*, Cecil (4)
5 *Dartmoor (3)*, (4) Hayward
6 *Follow the (4)*, John (6)
7 *Boundary (7) On and Around Dartmoor*, Dave (6)
8 *Dartmoor (6)*, Rufus (5)
9 *Dartmoor (11)*, (4) Swinscow
10 *(4) Dartmoor*, Eric (6)
11 *(6) Dartmoor*, (3) Tullett
12 *My (4) of the Moor*, John (7)
13 *Dartmoor (4)*, (3) Quick
14 *The (1) to (1) of Dartmoor (4)*, Terry (5)
15 *To Tavistock (6, 4)*, Clive (7)
16 *Dartmoor's (8) Walk*, Bill (6)
17 *The (5) of Dartmoor*, David (4)
18 *The (7) Way*, Derek (6)
19 *Bovey Tracey an (7) Town*, Lance (9)
20 *(8) in the Water*, Bob (7)

60. Learned about Lustleigh?

1 In which year was the first *Small Talk at Wreyland* published?
2 What non 'Small Talk' book had Cecil Torr previously written?
3 What did Major Graham try to retrieve in 1950?
4 Whose *System of Divinity*, which ran to hundreds of pages, was printed by himself but proved a big disappointment as it provoked little response from those who counted?

5 On which branch line did the village station stand?

6 What is the Parson's Loaf?

7 James Nutcombe Gould was a villager on the verge of fame and fortune when he died but in which sphere?

8 What is the name of the gallery and gift shop in the village?

9 In which open space are May Queens crowned?

10 What was the name of the station changed to for the benefit of a 1930s film based on a Dartmoor legend?

61. Mugged-up on Moretonhampstead?

1 What was the nickname of the extremely clever George Parker Bidder who was born in 1806 at Moreton?

2 What were other names given to the once-famous Cross Tree?

3 Which Down, to the north-east of the town, rises to over 1100 feet above sea level?

4 What is now located on the site of the former railway station?

5 What is the name of the gallery in Moreton, one of the earliest to display Brian Carter's wildlife paintings?

6 To which saint is the parish church dedicated?

7 What happened, in 1826, to the house where Parker Bidder was born?

8 What words were reputedly painted on the town's gasometer during the war?

9 What is the name of the hamlet between Steps Bridge and Moretonhampstead?

10 What type of probably reluctant visitor arrived in the town on 23 January 1807?

62. Dartmoor Dates

1 Which church, built by prisoners of war, celebrated its first service on 2 January 1814?
2 Which famous vicar of Lewtrenchard died 2 January 1924?
3 Which Dartmoor farm was first lit by electricity on 4 January 1893?
4 Where was a foundation stone laid on 5 January 1907 whilst the building started was not completed until 1932?
5 Which celebrated Tavistock authoress died on 21 January 1893?
6 Why was 24 January 1932 a memorable day in the life of Princetown?
7 Which ancient group of stones collapsed on 31 January 1862?
8 (Below) Who was shot dead in Chagford on 8 February 1643?

9 Which former youth hostel and fine home, to the south of the Avon Dam, was demolished by Royal Marines on 16 February 1968?
10 Which abbey was dissolved on 3 March 1539?
11 Which branch line saw its last passengers on 5 March 1956?
12 (Below) What happened at the Moorland Hotel, near Haytor, on 6 March 1970?

13 What began on 9 March 1891?
14 Which pub changed its name on 1 April 1984, having previously been called the Yelverton Hotel and the Foxhunter?
15 Which Dartmoor National Trust property had its foundation stone laid on 4 April 1911?
16 Which Dartmoor writer collapsed and died whilst out walking near his Clearbrook home on 7 April 1986?
17 Which Elizabethan dramatist was christened at Ilsington church on 12 April 1586?

18 On which Dartmoor tor did the last 'Point to Point' take place on 25 April 1951?
19 Which stannary town saw the arrival of the railways on 1 April 1872?
20 Which Cornish writer visited Cranmere Pool, with the Launceston Hiking Club, on 5 May 1938?
21 Where did Ruth St Leger-Gordon open a new box on 8 May 1935?

22 Which famous logan stone was pushed down a hillside on 11 May 1950?
23 Which Mayor of Okehampton, who is associated with a Cranmere Pool legend, died on 22 May 1701?
24 In which newspaper did the first William Crossing article appear on 2 June 1900?
25 Which Dartmoor reservoir, supplying the Torbay area, opened on 22 June 1942?
26 Which famous Dartmoor writer died at Newton Abbot Hospital on 3 July 1955?
27 Which river demolished Hill Bridge on 5 July 1880?
28 What happened to Jonathan May at Jacob's Well, near Moretonhampstead, on 16 July 1835?
29 Which church was gutted by fire on 20 July 1992?
30 Where did Arthur Clement begin chiselling a biblical text on 23 July 1928?
31 Which famous musician landed at RAF Harrowbeer, Yelverton, on 28 August 1944, the same year that 'he went missing'.
32 On 29 August 1894 Dartmoor's most elusive letterbox was signed for the first time but which one was it?
33 Which settlement became the first to have streets lit by electric light on 1 September 1891?
34 Which Dartmoor railroad and mineral line opened on 11 September 1911?
35 Which other mineral line, to carry granite, opened 17 September 1820?
36 Which vicar and poet was buried at Dean Prior Church on 15 October 1674?
37 Who called at the Tavistock Inn on 21 October 1638?
38 Which 'letterbox' opened on 23 October 1938?
39 Who presented a window to Princetown's church on 4 June 1910?
40 Which Dartmoor reservoir, to serve Paignton, opened on 26 June 1907?

63. Who Am I, Again?

1   I have lived near Throwleigh and have presented television programmes but most will know me for my 'black and white' photography of Dartmoor characters.

2   I am a famous actor, born in 1908 and father of a famous film actress, who came to Dartmoor in 1969 to film *Run Wild, Run Free*.

3   I was once in television, then an MP and wrote a number of books including *The Magic of Dartmoor*.

4   I live in Dartmoor and I appear in many comedy programmes. My fellow female compatriot is a Plymouth girl who is also married to a comedian.

5   (Right) I presented many television programmes, including *Cobblestones, Cottages and Castles*, which featured Dartmoor and was always seen with my faithful Labrador companion.

See Question 5

6   I invented the jet engine and spent a lot of time at Chagford.

7   I was once editor of *Devon Life* and have written many novels as well as local books which include *Along the Teign, Along the Lemon* and *Tales of the Unexplained in Devon* to name but a few.

8   I once dressed up as a sheep to get a close-up photo of a fox! I had a great interest in wildlife and was based at Cheston near South Brent.

9   I started walking Dartmoor at a grand old age and continued for many years. One of my major projects was the book *Following the Leat*.

10   Along with my wife, Hilary, I have written several books about Okehampton. Cricket is my passion and in recent years I have been heavily involved with Chagford's cricket club.

11   I am a regular writer in the *Herald Express* and have written much about walking in the countryside. I presented a series of four programmes about the different seasons on Dartmoor, called *The Threatened Wilderness*.

12   I was married to Tom, who was an ostler at the Two Bridges Hotel and together we built Jolly Lane Cot, the last house to be built in a day on Dartmoor. When I died, at a grand old age, I was given the honour of having a 'carrying funeral' to my last resting place in Widecombe.

13   I lived at Grenofen, on the banks of the Walkham, for many years. After being a news reporter I entered television as a newsreader and I have presided over quiz shows. I was in a *Morecambe and Wise Show* and I have long legs!

14   I was one of the first sports reporters, along with David Vine, for Westward TV and I was also the owner of the Cabin, a cafe at Leg o' Mutton, Yelverton.

15   I appear as a number of statues in Devon, one is on Plymouth Hoe, the other near my native Tavistock.

16   In Victorian times I spent a lot of time taking photographs of Dartmoor and I was a founder member of the Dartmoor Preservation Association.

17   I am a titled lady who lives at Cator and who loves Dartmoor. My grandfather was Robert Burnard.

18 I am just a pair of limbs deemed responsible for a number of road accidents between Postbridge and Cherry Brook Bridge.

19 I was, for many years, a television weatherman. I have written for a number of newspapers and have 'fronted' many radio programmes for BBC Radio Devon. I lived near Lee Moor for a number of years but have since moved closer to sea level!

20 In the late 1990s I was in the news a lot because I was 'kidnapped' many times from my home at the Dartmoor View Caravan Park at Whiddon Down. However I was usually returned and often by taxi. I'm the handsome, irresistible one in the picture!

See Question 20

21 I am missing from this line-up: Bill Brewer, Jan Stewer, Peter Gurney, Dan'l Whiddon, Harry Hawk, Old Uncle Tom Cobley and all!

22 I lived on the moor in my youth and later became a famous actor. I loved fly fishing and filmed some angling scenes with Harry Secombe at Bellever.

23 I, too, filmed some fishing scenes for television but at Prince Hall. I live at Lyme Regis and am a singer and comedian.

24 I, too, filmed on Dartmoor for a legendary series for the BBC. There were no daleks around but near Haytor I fell and broke my collar bone.

25 I once described Dartmoor as one of the most dangerous parts of the British Isles on account of its quick-changing weather. I am a famous climber and, although I have climbed in Devon, I am better known for scaling the world's loftiest mountains.

26 I appeared in a film made in the Tavistock area but am more famous for my part in an American detective series with my colleague 'Starsky'.

27 I was buried at Buckfastleigh but managed to escape my grave to roam the moors once more. Conan Doyle knew of me and my dark deeds.

28 I was a librarian in Plymouth for many years and did a series of radio broadcasts about the South Devon coastline and a series on television called *Attic Archives*. One of my books was about the place-names of Dartmoor and the Plymouth area.

29 I narrated a television series about Dartmoor in the late 1990s but am better-known for going 'Walkabout' in Australia in 1970.

30 When I was a Teignmouth coach driver I drove passengers to Dartmoor as often as I could because I loved the moors. Many will remember the watering can I kept in the coach for playing as a musical instrument. You can see a photo of me in Chips Barber's *Diary of a Devonshire Walker*.

31 I was the last keeper at Dunnabridge Pound and Mr Hansford Worth kindly photographed me sat in the 'Judge's Chair' there but that was a long time ago!

32 I was the Lord of the Manor of Spitchwick in the late nineteenth century and was responsible for the building of a carriageway around some of the upper slopes of the Dart Gorge.

33 I was the vicar of Sheepstor from 1 November 1907 and became so interested in the moor that I started writing books about it. Later I was vicar of Dean Prior.

34 I was a poor girl who became pregnant out of wedlock. Out of shame I went into a barn at Canna and hanged myself. They buried me at a nearby crossroads and there are always fresh flowers at my grave.

35 I wrote books about Devon's ghosts and the paranormal including one about Postbridge and district which appeared under the title *Tales of a Dartmoor Village*, published in 1961. I was heavily involved with that wonderful 'institution', the Devonshire Association and wrote many papers for them when I was the folklore secretary.

36 (Right) I once appeared on television sat on a giant mushroom telling stories of pixies, which earned me the title 'Dartmoor's leading Pixiecologist'! My third book was *Diary of a Dartmoor Walker* and, despite my name, it's not my ambition to open my own hairdresser shop!

37 I shared that same mushroom at Pixieland and was the presenter of the series in which the feature appeared.

38 I was mildly critical of Lustleigh in my book *Devon Villages* and am best known for my books about Exmoor. I was a teacher at Blundell's School for several years.

39 I was married to Sally and was once an ostler at the Two Bridges Hotel. With friends we once built a house in a day!

40 I live in Ashburton and have been a Portreeve but most will know me better for my voice and the way I speak as I am a keen exponent of the Devonshire dialect. 'See you dreckly!?'

See Questions 36 and 37

64. Help! Where Am I?

1 I can see the two churches of St Marychurch and also the clay waste heaps at St Austell. Below me is one of the moor's most austere buildings. If I climbed a nearby man-made structure I would be the highest person in Devon.

2 (Below) I am on a 'tor', a common name on the moor, which is not granite and in a wooded gorge. I can see away to my right a National Trust property. But I should apologise because I took this picture before it was built!

3 I am close to a large circle and on the northern branch of a river. I am inside a peculiar stone which I am told has curing qualities for those who suffer rheumatism.

4 I am on a bridge where four parishes meet and which gives its name to the village, which has recently grown into a small town.

5 I am on a 'submarine' high on southern Dartmoor, but this one has never been to sea as it's only a barrow that resembles one when seen from certain angles.

6 I am in a pub which used to boast the rudest landlord in the country. I am at a crossroads where Drogo lies in one direction and Chagford in the other.

7   (Below) I am at a pool between Cranmere and OP15.

8   I am stood on a hill just above White Slade (Snaily House) looking across the East Dart valley towards Laughter Tor.
9   I am stood on a high point about three quarters of mile almost due west of Cranmere Pool.
10 I am stood at the top of a tor which has a staircase leading to its summit.
11 I am surrounded by ruins, in particular chimneys. The Cherry Brook trundles by.
12 I am stood in a not very desirable detached ruin very close to the top of Winney's Down.
13 I am in a well-known hotel, at an important Dartmoor crossroads, which has a Vivienne Leigh suite.
14 I am surrounded by ceramic footballers who really ought to be playing for Cranmere Rovers as they specialise in getting people lost on the moor or making them dance until they drop!

See Question 19

15 I am not in Australia, although my name has antipodean tendencies. I am on a lovely tor overlooking the Walkham valley.
16 I am on a small tor about half a mile to the west of Wind Tor where the guide Dr Malim is remembered by a small plaque.
17 I am on a hill, with many fine outcrops, which used to have a golf course on it but now has a fine football and cricket pitch at the bottom of it. Mr Webber, a trader in a nearby settlement, still has an old sign for the course, and Luke Darlington once tried to play a round on it, losing many balls in the process.
18 I am sat by a cross on a small rock which is a memorial to a young man killed in the First World War.
19 I am on a high rockpile (as depicted on some of the tiles in Princetown's public conveniences!) on private land but with public access. There are no witches around me today.
20 I am on a tor of curious appearance which has featured in the opening sequences of a local evening television news programme for several years. I can see a fine set of ruins of a medieval village close-by.

65. More Dartmoor Railways

If you suffer from 'Anoraksia Nervosa', beware!

1 Who wrote *Iron Horse to the Sea*?
2 And who wrote the foreword to this 1987 book?
3 What is the initial letter of railway writer Anthony Kingdom's middle name?
4 What was the name of the crossing at Dousland which later became the site of the post office and stores?
5 Which major moorland hotel was bought by the GWR in 1929 and developed into a major golfing venue?
6 Which South Dartmoor town has a 'Park and Ride' station?
7 Where was there a 869-yard-long tunnel on the Exeter–Plymouth line?
8 At which railway station did Anna Neagle and Rex Harrison shoot scenes for *I Live in Grosvenor Square*?
9 How many miles long was the Moretonhampstead & South Devon Railway when it opened?
10 Which town with a railway station was described as being 12 miles from everywhere, this including Exeter, Newton Abbot, Crediton and Okehampton?

66. Briefed on Bovey Tracey?

1 Where did Major Hole live?
2 Which two comedians filmed at the Major Hole's home after his death?
3 Who wrote two books about Bovey, the second being *Bovey Tracey in Bygone Days* published in 1989?
4 What is the generally more accepted term for 'Bovey coal'?
5 To whom is the parish church dedicated?
6 What were Royalist officers supposedly doing when Cromwell surprised them on 9 January 1646 during the English Civil War?
7 Whose cave is found within Furzeleigh Rocks, about a mile from the town?
8 Which company makes teapots and 'caused quite a stir', even 'a storm in a teacup', when 'nearly-nude models', as shown, appeared on the roof of their premises?
9 What are Prince Albert, Old William, Old Jack and Victoria?

See Question 8

10 What did Mr T. Hydon of Bovey Pottery make 70,000 of, using some 50 tons of ball clay from mines in mid-Devon and Dorset, and china clay from St Austell, in the first half of 1953?
11 After whom is an arch in Bovey named?
12 What used to be held on the first Monday after 3rd May at Bovey Tracey?
13 What were the Portreeves' Parks?
14 Where was there once a hospital which cared for tuberculosis sufferers?
15 Why were Eureka Terrace and Spion Kop (Mary Street) so named?
16 Which Devon dialect expert was once a schoolteacher in the town?
17 Until 1910 the old Grammar School stood beside the road to Haytor but what is it now?
18 What was built and opened on the site of the former village green?
19 The old Bridge House was once owned by a man whose name had a distinctly biblical feel to it. Bearing in mind the way the Bovey could rise very quickly after a downpour what was his name?
20 What is the name of the bridge, on the old A38, spanning the Bovey?

67. Map Knowledge – Taw Country

Name the tors at 1, 2, 3, 4 and 5, the marsh at 6, the wall at 7, the river at 8, the stream at 9 and the farm at 10.

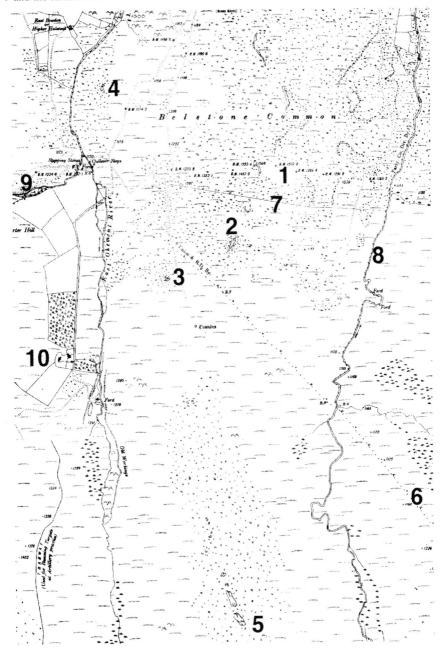

68. Laid-back about Lydford?

1 Who owns and manages Lydford Gorge?
2 What were the band of ruffians who once lived in the gorge?
3 What is the name of the pub in the centre of the village?
4 Which MP was held in Lydford's notorious prison by the tinners?
5 What does 'Lyd' probably mean?
6 What is the name of the high waterfall in Lydford Gorge?
7 What profession did George Routleigh follow?
8 Which 'tor' is found in Lydford Gorge?
9 To which saint is Lydford's lovely church dedicated?
10 Whose 'steps' , on the Lyd, lie a short distance east of the village?

69. Tavistock Teasers

1 Which well-known snooker player hails from Tavistock?
2 What were the first names of the founder of Kelly College?
3 Where was the birthplace of Drake?
4 Which green Hurdwick stone building was the work of Jacob Saunders in 1720?

5 In 1976 it was deemed necessary to lay down granite setts in the vicinity of the pannier market but from where was this granite obtained?
6 Which two famous Second World War 'characters' met at Abbotsfield Hall to make arrangements for the D Day landings?
7 Prior to 1846 where did horse races take place?
8 Who went to Goozey Fair with 'me' according to the folk song?
9 Which three friends did they meet up with in Tavistock?
10 Where did the duo have problems on the return journey?

70. Map Knowledge – Bovey Country

Name the tors at 1 and 2, the former Corn Mill at 3, the outcrop at 4, the 3 Cleaves at 5, 6 and 7, the former Logan Stone at 8, the beauty spot at 9 and the Steps at 10.

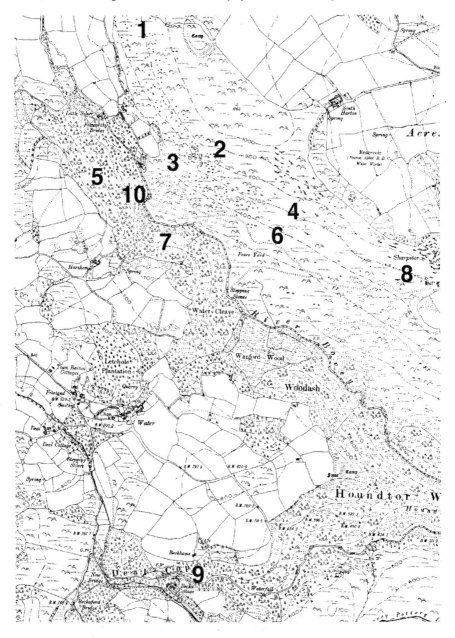

71. An A-Z of Dartmoor Tors – but Which Tors … ?

Here are 23 tors/rocks/hills, which the first letter given as a starting point, for you to identify on an A-Z basis. (Yes, I know there are 26 letters in the alphabet but for once it's not 'z' which is the problem in trying to get a full sequence!)

1   **A** – is for a tor visible from the Postbridge–Cherry Brook bridge road.
2   **B** – is for a tor accessed via a gate near the lower car park at Haytor and lies close to a mill which takes its name from it.
3   **C** – is for a tor (below), just outside the metamorphic aureole, which affords fine views of the Tavistock countryside and into Cornwall.

4   **D** – is for a rocky, craggy mass in the Plym valley between Cadover and Shaugh bridges.
5   **E** – is for a hill which possesses a line of PCWW stones and workers once toiled at Wheal Ruth here.
6   **F** – is for a tor whose shape and appearance its name reflects.
7   **G** – is for a tor that overlooks Bleak House.
8   **H** – is for a tor near Postbridge very close to where a Warrington-based teacher was once found dead, who is remembered by a small memorial.
9   **I** – is for a tor on the edge of Skaigh Warren in the Taw valley.
10 **K** – is for a distinctive rock which has its name shared by a pub many miles from it and a fine rock basin.
11 **L** – is for a tor of good fortune which almost rivals Vixen Tor in its height.
12 **M** – is for a tor in the vicinity of Frenchbeer Rock and Thornworthy Tor.
13 **N** – is for a tor in the Tavy valley.
14 **O** – is for a tiny and obscure tor which is seen from the path which passes Bernard's Acre and which has the Taw flowing nearby.
15 **P** – is for a tor (below) which has been spelt two distinctive ways, either with two or three letters but please don't kick up a stink as to which is right! Stone from here was used in nearby Tavistock and, sadly, ponies were killed during the Second World War when a warplane discharged its load.

16 **R** – is for a tor in name, which has no significant rock mass. Its small rocks can be located about 300 yards from East Rook Gate above Cornwood.

17 **S** – is for a small pile in the Throwleigh area and close to a road and the Forder Brook.

18 **T** – is for a tor close to Fernworthy Reservoir and not far from Frenchbeer Rock.

19 **U** – is for an outcrop on the southern edge of the National Park, one which is matched by a village prettier than its name a few miles to the south of it.

20 **V** – is a for tor which might fox you!

21 **W** – is for a tor with a Thurlestone or holed rock.

22 **Y** – is for a lofty tor in the affirmative (above).

23 **Z** – is for a tor in name only.

72. Map Knowledge – Lyd Country

Can you name the tors 1, 2 and 3, the streams 4, 5 and 6, the cross at 7, the Down at 8, the hill at 9 and the Gate at 10?

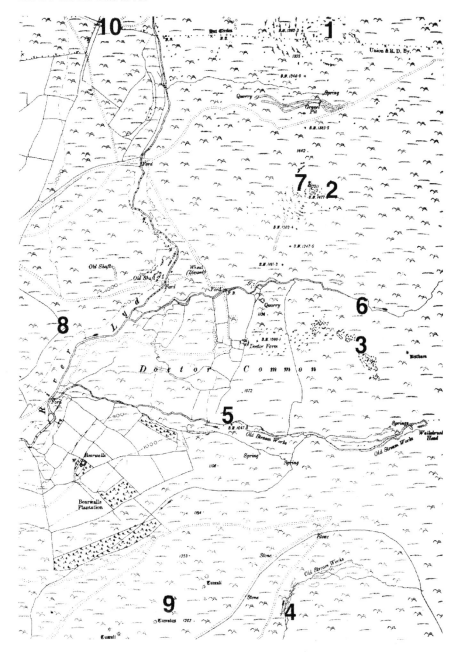

73. One Hundred and Eighty 'Moor' Questions

(with some absolute 'snorters' sneaked in just to finish you off!)

1. Which well-known Irish singer recorded a song called 'Dartmoor'?
2. Whose elbow used to cause problems near Princetown?
3. Which unusual animals have been kept at Two Bridges for many years?
4. Where would you find the Heath Stone?
5. Near which bridge does the Pipe Track begin?
6. What two colours are found on the range boundary markers?
7. Who did the sketches for F. H. (Harry) Starkey's early Dartmoor books?
8. Who did the sketches for *Crossing's Guide to Dartmoor*?
9. In which Eden Phillpotts story did a Scotch beast attack Nicholas Edgecombe near Devil's Tor?
10. Where were Fowler, Marshall, Dixon, Wale, Stumpy the Weaver and Pot-Bellied Gale going in a folk song?
11. (Right) Which building in Widecombe houses Tom Cobley's Chair?
12. What are Cranbrook, Prestonbury and Wooston?
13. Beside which stream was Kit Tin Mine?
14. What name, according to William Crossing, was always given for a menhir on the moor?
15. Who wrote the well-known rhyme about 'Lydford Law'?
16. For what was 'mort gabel' a payment?
17. What was supposed to be the size of a newtake, excepting rocks and bogs?
18. Which of Dartmoor's sepulchral circles is the largest?
19. What was the name of the former road between Okehampton and Tavistock?
20. Which ancient track runs up the right bank of the East Dart from Postbridge?
21. According to Crossing, once more, on which tor would you find 'Mrs Bray's Wash-hand Basin'?
22. In which ancient wood, in the nineteenth century, was Sam Adams' terrier, Jumbo, buried? (It's now an SSSI!)
23. What is the only 'Down' on Dartmoor to start with a 'z'?
24. What was the nearest tor to Billy Clack's Cottage? (Before the National Park boundaries were established this tor was believed to be the centre of the moor.)
25. How many rock basins are found atop Vixen Tor?
26. (Right) Where did Mrs Ashplant start a tea shelter which later blossomed into a grander establishment?

(Above) See Question 11

(Below) See Question 26

27 Which uniquely located Dartmoor church was re-consecrated by Bishop Stapeldon on 4 December 1319?

28 In which valley was Forest Mine?

29 What was mined at Ramsley above South Zeal?

30 What name now appears on the map instead of 'Crovenor Steps'?

31 Which former Dartmoor National Park chief was a lecturer at St Luke's College in Exeter?

32 Which Down lies beside the road between Swallerton Gate and Jay's Grave?

33 In which hamlet would you find St Raphael's Chapel?

34 Which Dartmoor village was once famous for its Ram Roast?

35 Who or what once owned Holne Moor, Buckfastleigh Moor and Brent Moor?

36 Crossing wrote of a tiny beauty spot called 'Henchertraw'. On which stream was it found?

37 What does 'traw' mean?

38 What were natives of Ilsington called?

39 What was needed to set the Rugglestone rocking?

40 Which watercourse is spanned by Runnage Bridge?

41 (Below) Beside which river is there a granite cross to the memory of young Christopher Holman Richards who drowned in it in the 1920s?

42 In which Dartmoor village was there once a pub called the Greyhound Inn?

43 Who wrote the novel *Classywell's Secret*?

44 What do Tom Tullett, Rufus Endle, George Dendrickson and Fred Thomas all have in common?

45 What pseudonym did Eric Hemery adopt for a walking book in the 1980s?

46 Which beam runs from Snowdon Hole down to the Western Wella Brook?

47 How did George Stephens, who 'sleeps' in a lonely moorland grave, die?

48 Which hill rises immediately above the Warren House Inn?

49 Which inn, that no longer exists, was built in the 1830s to serve nearby granite quarry workers? It was replaced by the Prince of Wales Inn in nearby Princetown and this 'terrace' (below), which has since been restored, is close by.

50 A cylindrical stone of red granite is found at Trowlesworthy Tor. Some say it was intended as a podium to go at the top of a column. To which 'newly-named' town was it meant to go?

51 The stone was cut in 1824 so which monarch's statue was intended to be mounted on it?

52 To which church does Elbow Lane lead?

53 What important organisation was the brainchild of Bill Ames in 1968?

54 Which leat, constructed in 1859, carried water from the River Swincombe to the Mardle to supplement the flow in order to drive waterwheels at Brookwood?

55 Which Falklands war hero 'started' the 32nd Ten Tors Expedition?

56 In which year did the 32nd Expedition take place?

57 From which town did the original waterwheel and tilt hammers of the Finch Foundry, Sticklepath, come?

58 Which tor, to the south of Devil's Bridge, once had a rifle range leading up to it?

59 Who wrote *The Dartmoor Mountain Bike Guide*?

60 What do Chagford, Morwellham Quay and Mary Tavy have in common?

61 Whose well lies on the slopes of Wittaburrow close to Blackslade Water?

62 What were the middle names of Eric Hemery, the celebrated Dartmoor writer?

63 Who carved the wooden fish found on the walls of the Anglers Rest at Fingle Bridge?

64 Which author of travel books, who spent much of her childhood in and around Chagford, had her 100th birthday on 31 January 1993?

65 Where did a Dakota crash on 13 October 1945 killing its crew of seven American airmen?

66 Which river is crossed at Chalk Ford?

67 Which 'house' is located about half a mile to the north-west of Lower White Tor?

68 What is the full name of the man after whom this house is named?

69 What was the main title of Elizabeth Stanbrook's book which was subtitled *A Social History from Enclosure to Abandonment*?

70   (Below) Which clapper bridge is supposedly the work of William Rogers?

71   When did the Two Moors Way officially open?
72   What was a more popular name for Swincombe Ford Cottage?
73   Which river was spanned by 'Trena Bridge'?
74   What is the name of the clapper bridge over the Blackbrook which carried the old
      packhorse road from Moreton to Plymouth?
75   Which religious and 'concise' family camped at Huntingdon Warren in the early years
      of the twentieth century? One of the sons was into 'flora' but not the margarine!
76   At Bovey there is 'Indio' marked on the map. What does it probably mean?
77   Which tower, on private land near Chagford, shares a name with a wood, a mill, a bridge
      and stepping stones (below) across the Teign?

78   What is the name of the folly at Gidleigh Tor?
79   Which river does Fish Lake join?
80   Which stream 'falls into the Dart in Buckland Woods'?
81   Which river does Ponsworthy Bridge span?

82   (Below) Of what were Thomas Windeatt's workmen responsible for the demolition?

83   How many miles is it from one end to the other of the Two Moors Way?
84   If L9 is Wistman's Wood, and Powder Mills L10, then what is L11? (365 is a clue!)
85   Which packhorse bridge spanning the Bovey has a granite gate post beside it?
86   Near which river did the Liverpudlian William Donaghy die in 1914?
87   In 1608 which tor replaced Limsboro Cairn as the named point on the Forest boundary?
88   On which river would you find Cataloo Steps?
89   What was mined at Great Rock Mine, near Hennock?
90   What does the year '1954' carved on a stone in the Town Orchard at Lustleigh signify?
91   On which estate would you find 'the Three Fishes' stones?
92   What are the three inscriptions on these stones?
93   What is another name for the Whooping Rock?
94   Which warren was sited between Spanish Lake and Hentor Brook?
95   Who forged the peat pass through Black Ridge?
96   Which single word precedes all of the following: Down, Cottages, House, Woods and Mill?
97   What are the next 3 letters: 1A, 2R, 3R, 4E, 5H, 6T, 7O, 8M, 9M?
98   (Below) On which village green are there trees planted to commemorate 'Royal' occasions?

99   Which bridge on the Teign, between Fingle and Steps bridges has a caravan site beside it?
100 Where did the West of England Compressed Peat Company once cut peat?

101 Where would you find Maximager's Stone?

102 Whose 'grave' lies a short way uphill from Maximager's Stone?

103 What is the name of the nine-arched viaduct built to carry the railway along the edge of the moor between Okehampton and Tavistock?

104 (Right) What is the name of the junction of the B3212 and the road from Manaton close to Beetor Cross?

105 Who go to Roost close to Sherwell?

106 Which pool lies near the start of the Red-a-ven Brook?

107 On which hill is there a stone row known as 'The Graveyard'?

108 Which Dartmoor reservoir opened in 1972?

109 Which viaduct spans the East Okement near Okehampton?

(Above) See Question 104

110 (Above) Which reservoir does the Brockhill Stream fall into?

111 Which river was also known as the Mew?

112 Where was 'Will May's House'?

113 Who had a lane named after him, having regularly carried peat from Dinger Plain to Knack/Knock Mine?

114 Who excavated Roundy Pound in 1952?

115 Beside which stream is Bush Down found on its upper right bank?

116 What was Yard Gate once known as?

117 Where would you find Cathanger Rock?

118 Which settlement did Gregory Wall write a portrait of ?

119 After passing through Coffin Wood which appropriately-named lane is met?

120 Which stream rises near Crockern Tor and falls into the Cherry Brook at Lower Cherrybrook Bridge?

121 Which stream is crossed by Pizwell Steps?

122 Which stream runs between Great Combe Tor and Little Combe Tor?

123 (Below) What was the name of the pub which was once found in the centre of Manaton?

124 Which moorland-edge town did Hemery describe as " … a pleasant, miniature town, compact and practically unspoilt."?

125 Numerically, which Commando outfit are based at Bickleigh?

126 What is the Dry Rock at Yelverton?

127 What is the name of the village pub at Shaugh Prior?

128 What did the original Shaugh Prior pub, of this name, have in common with the Warren House Inn?

129 Which stream is spanned by Saddle Bridge?

130 Which river has its source at 'Big Head'?

See Question 138

131 What are sometimes known as the 'Cornwood Maidens'?

132 Which railway runs past Sammy Thompson's Cottage?

133 Where would you find 'the Northwest Passage' on Dartmoor?

134 What is a Dartmoor equivalent of Will o'the Wisp?

135 Which Cornwood family had boundary stones bearing their initial?

136 Which gentle hill lies between the car park on Pork Hill and Feather Tor?

137 Which parish has a boundary stone between Higher and Lower Dunnagoat?

138 (Right) What is the name of the place where this memorial is found?

139 Beside which river was Wheal Fortune?
140 Where did a spalliard work?
141 Which road leads from Princetown to Peat Cot?
142 On which river is Travellers' Ford?
143 What was the name of the pre-1817 road from Tavistock to Okehampton?
144 (Below) From where was the Judge's Chair at Dunnabridge said to have been brought?

145 On which hill were fires once supposedly seen at night, 'lighted by the Evil One' who keeps a wary eye on the feuding men of Okehampton and Tavistock?

146 What began on Dartmoor in 1873 and still continues?

See Question 147

147 (Right) According to Crossing, again, which place was he describing when he wrote: "hardly deserves the name of a village, consisting as it does, only of a church, a school, an ancient manor house, now a farm, and a few dwellings. These are grouped round a green on which is a fine old tree and an ancient cross. It is a restful place, and although some recent erections have somewhat marred its primitive aspect, it has by no means entirely lost its old-world appearance."?

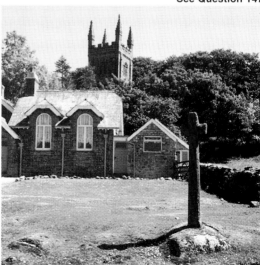

148 What regular users of Dartmoor had their 'organisation' founded on 28 October 1664?

149 Which down rises just to the north of Ivybridge?

150 What is the name of the pub, up a steep slope, in the hamlet of Lutton near Cornwood?

151 (Pic 1) What is the present name for a place which was referred to in Victorian times as 'the hamlet of Heytor Town'.

152 Near which village is Fernworthy Down?

153 In the past where was Dartmeet School housed?

154 Where was Walkhampton Foggintor School located?

155 According to William Crossing which path 'leads from Brent Tor to the Rattle Brook'?

156 Which two parts of the anatomy go with the name Kneeset?

157 To which tor is Windy Cross close?

158 (Pic 2) In which wood would you find this section of the Haytor Granite Tramway?

159 What was Crossing's book *The Teign* sub-titled?

160 Who wrote *Christowell* which featured the Cross Tree at Moretonhampstead?

161 Which distinctive rock lies just under a mile to the north-west of Blackingstone Rock?

162 (Pic 3) What is the name of this small clapper bridge?

163 In which valley would you find Whiddon Wood and Butterdon Ball Wood?

164 Which wood is found on the spur of land where the Becka Brook joins the Bovey?

165 (Pic 4) On which rock would you find 'the Duke of Wellington's nose' as shown in this photograph?

166 (Below) Jane Hayter-Haymes wrote a book about it and so did Terry Bound and Chips Barber, but which place is this?

167 Which is the odd one out and why: Buttern Hill, Rough Tor, Fox Tor, Nine Stones, Sharp Tor and High Willhays?

168 This picture below shows a crossing place on the River Lyd but what is the name of the distinct hill, used by hang glider enthusiasts, in the background?

169 (Below) Test Match cricket rarely comes to Dartmoor but here you have living proof that the occasional match graces the moor. Here is a roadside cricket arena, where there is the odd 'Splash', a few miles from Widecombe but what is the name of the hamlet where this ancient and traditional English game is taking place in miniature?

170 On which moor to coast walk would you pass Stover Lake?

171 Beside which river is Halstock Wood?

172 (Right) This picture shows a wonderful waterfall above Hawns and Dendles. The river gathers momentum as it wends its way to pass 'Mother Hubbard's Cottage' and Kitley Caves, before reaching the sea beyond Newton and Noss, but which one is it?

173 Who wrote *Dartmoor Letterboxes* and *More Dartmoor Letterboxes*?

174 Where, on the moor, did carpenters build a wooden 'Camelot' for the 1953 film *Knights of the Round Table* starring Robert Taylor and Ava Gardner?

175 (Below) This bridge helped to inspire an 'Edwardian Diary' but what is the name of the bridge and which river does it span?

176 Which stream runs down Stony Bottom?

177 Which river flows through Lustleigh Cleave?

178 Where would you find Pearl's Cross?

179 How did Spanny save the nation?

See Question 180

180 Finally … At which Dartmoor car park do motorists manage to get their cars 'stranded' on a regular basis? (Or so the ice-cream salesman told me!)

After extensive research amongst both Dartmoor enthusiasts and quiz addicts, we have been assured that most people prefer **not** to have the answers readily to hand. By not putting the answers in the back of the book, we have also created maximum room for questions! However, when you reach that point of frustration when you really **have** to know, for your **FREE** set of **answer sheets** please send **a large stamped self-addressed envelope** to **Obelisk Publications, 2 Church Hill, Pinhoe, Exeter, Devon EX4 9ER** and we will put you out of your misery!